PRAISE FOR

THE PASSION TEST

"*The Passion Test* astounds us with the possibility that life can be fun, challenging, rewarding, and purposeful, all at the same time. Chris and Janet Attwood will take you on an adventure into your own heart and show you how to wake up the passions that are the fuel for living the life you were meant to live."

—Richard Paul Evans, #1 *New York Times*
bestselling author of *The Christmas Box*

"Quite frankly I was blown away. *The Passion Test* is a very direct, practical roadmap for how to become prosperous, how to take what it is you love and make it into a very, very substantial and very fulfilling income."

—Bill Harris, director of
Centerpointe Research Institute and featured in *The Secret*™

"*The Passion Test* is very provocative and very revealing, and it's unlike anything anyone has ever exposed me to. It challenged me in a very telling way."

—Jay Abraham, marketing genius and author of
Getting Everything You Can Out of All You've Got

"From a neurological perspective, The Passion Test™ is a powerful and compassionate tool that will help you to focus and strengthen your brain so that you can realize your innermost dreams."

—Mark Waldman, associate fellow at the
Center for Spirituality and the Mind, University of Pennsylvania
and coauthor of *Born to Believe*

"I want everybody to take The Passion Test. As an outcome of coaching people for three decades I have learned that lasting success begins with discovering, staying connected to, and getting good at your passions. Some of the things you will become passionate about may not even have been invented yet—so reading this book and taking The Passion Test several times a year will keep you connected and on track. Please give yourself the gift of the passionate life."

—Stewart Emery, coauthor of *Success Built to Last*

"I couldn't put it down. The story is so engaging, I almost forgot how much I wanted to take the Test. Then, taking the Test, I realized how valuable it was to hear Janet's story and what she went through to get to the point where she could live her passion."

—Yehuda Berg, the Kabbalah Centre and
author of *The 72 Names of God, The Power of Kabbalah,* and
The Red String Book

"*The Passion Test* has you focus on those things that are most important in your life, and passion is one of the keys to success for anyone, anywhere in the world. *The Passion Test* will be valuable for me, as the founder of BNI, in understanding what my franchisees are passionate about, because if they're not passionate about the things they're doing, they can have all the ability in the world, but they're not going to be as successful at running the programs we want them to run as they can be."

—Ivan Misner, chairman and founder of
BNI (Business Networks International)

"Simple, clear, powerful. *The Passion Test* is a remarkable tool for getting the clarity you need to begin living your dreams."
—Marci Shimoff, coauthor of the #1 *New York Times* bestsellers
Chicken Soup for the Woman's Soul and
Chicken Soup for the Mother's Soul

"Whether your life purpose is clear or you want to be clearer, *The Passion Test* provides a powerful tool for putting you on track to a more fulfilled, more complete life. The clearer your passions—the surer are your chances of realizing them."
—Dr. Pankaj Naram, world-renowned Ayurvedic physician and
coauthor of *Secrets of Natural Health*

"The Test itself is an incredibly valuable tool for clarifying what's really important to you in your life. Equally valuable were the lessons Chris and Janet Attwood share for actually living your mission."
—Catherine Lanigan, author of
Romancing the Stone and *Jewel of the Nile*

"There's absolutely no reason why everyone can't have the life they choose. You can create your life exactly as you want, but not if you're sacrificing your life's energy for something other than what you're most passionate about. I haven't found any process that will bring you absolutely to the place of your passion more quickly, more easily, and with more fun than The Passion Test."
—Paul Scheele, chairman of Learning Strategies Corporation

"I was amazed at the process—the simplicity and power of it. It has supported me in being much clearer in my daily priorities— brilliant!"

—D. C. Cordova, CEO and cofounder of
Excellerated Business Schools

"If you really want to have, do, be your passion—this is the guide for you. Janet and Chris have devised a powerful system that absolutely works!"
—Dr. Cheryl Clark, founder of Doing Life! International, Inc., and
director of Shock Incarceration and the Willard Drug Treatment
Campus, New York State Department of Correctional Services

"Great work Janet and Chris! Your fast-moving and illuminating book *The Passion Test* will certainly inspire its readers and help them discover and act upon their unique calling and mission as well as express their inner magnificence. I love the quotes, the stories, and the message. Thanks for helping us all do what is most important—live our heartfelt dreams."
—Dr. John F. Demartini, author of *The Breakthrough Experience:
A Revolutionary New Approach to Personal Transformation*,
featured in *The Secret*

"A wonderful and simple method for enabling your brain to help you embrace your beliefs in order to create your optimum reality."
—Andrew Newberg, associate professor of radiology and
psychiatry; director of the Center for Spirituality and the Mind,
University of Pennsylvania; and coauthor of *Born to Believe*

THE
PASSION
TEST

The Effortless Path
to Discovering Your
Destiny

JANET BRAY ATTWOOD
and
CHRIS ATTWOOD

HUDSON
STREET
PRESS

HUDSON STREET PRESS
Published by Penguin Group

Penguin Group (USA) Inc., 375 Hudson Street, New York, New York 10014, U.S.A. •
Penguin Group (Canada), 90 Eglinton Avenue East, Suite 700, Toronto, Ontario,
Canada M4P 2Y3 (a division of Pearson Penguin Canada Inc.) • Penguin Books Ltd.,
80 Strand, London WC2R 0RL, England • Penguin Ireland, 25 St. Stephen's Green,
Dublin 2, Ireland (a division of Penguin Books Ltd.) • Penguin Group (Australia),
250 Camberwell Road, Camberwell, Victoria 3124, Australia (a division of Pearson
Australia Group Pty. Ltd.) • Penguin Books India Pvt. Ltd., 11 Community Centre,
Panchsheel Park, New Delhi – 110 017, India • Penguin Group (NZ), 67 Apollo Drive,
Rosedale, North Shore 0632, New Zealand (a division of Pearson New Zealand Ltd.) •
Penguin Books (South Africa) (Pty.) Ltd., 24 Sturdee Avenue, Rosebank,
Johannesburg 2196, South Africa

Penguin Books Ltd., Registered Offices: 80 Strand, London WC2R 0RL, England

Published by Hudson Street Press, a member of Penguin Group (USA) Inc.
Previously published in a 1st World Publishing edition. For information address
1st World Publishing, 1100 North 4th Street, Suite 131, Fairfield, Iowa, 52556.

The Passion Test is a trademark of
Enlightened Alliances, LLC.

REGISTERED TRADEMARK—MARCA REGISTRADA

HUDSON
STREET
PRESS

ISBN-13: 978-0-7394-9439-4

Printed in the United States of America

PUBLISHER'S NOTE
The scanning, uploading, and distribution of this book via the Internet or via any other
means without the permission of the publisher is illegal and punishable by law. Please
purchase only authorized electronic editions, and do not participate in or encourage electronic piracy of copyrighted materials. Your support of the author's rights is appreciated.

Neither the publisher nor the authors are engaged in rendering financial, health, or
other professional advice or services to the individual reader. If you require such advice or
other expert assistance, you should seek the services of a competent professional. Nothing
in this book is intended as an express or implied warranty of the suitability or fitness of
any service or product. The reader wishing to use a service or product discussed in this
book should first consult a specialist or professional to ensure suitability and fitness for
the reader's particular needs. Neither the authors nor the publisher shall be liable or responsible for any loss or damage arising from any information or suggestion in this book.

While the authors have made every effort to provide accurate Internet and e-mail
addresses at the time of publication, neither the publisher nor the authors assume any
responsibility for errors, or for changes that occur after publication. Further, the publisher does not have any control over and does not assume any responsibility for author
or third-party websites or their content.

My Lord,
Thank you for every moment in our lives.
Thank you for all you have given us.
We are, because of you.
Whatever we do, think, have, or feel
Is because of you.
May we be vessels
Through which you speak.
Use us in ways you desire,
As your humble servants
Walking this path hand in hand with you.
May the words on these pages
Touch the hearts of all those yearning
For union with you.
May they inspire each of us
To align our lives with you and your will for us.
All we have,
We offer in gratitude.
We bow to you.

Contents

There are two great days
in a person's life—
the day we are born
and the day we discover why.
　　—*William Barclay*
　　　Scottish theologian
　　　and author, 1907–1978

Foreword

Do you ever feel discouraged and frustrated with your life? Do you ever feel like your dreams will never become reality? Well, this book will change that for you.

Who among us doesn't know that living our passion is the key to a happy and fulfilled life? The trick for many people, though, is figuring out what their passion really is.

I've often said, "The number one reason people don't get what they want is that they don't know what they want."

The Passion Test provides the simplest, clearest way to get started on knowing what you want—by getting clear on who you are. As you make your list of the ten or fifteen qualities of your ideal life, you'll be surprised to discover what it is that's really important to you.

Clarity is critical to success. Clarity leads to power—the power to act—which is the basis of achievement, fulfillment, and happiness in life. Without a clear direction you are either paralyzed or running around in circles. Worse, you can never reach your full potential because you dare not fully commit.

Not just any direction will do, and therein lies the challenge. Each of us is unique. Each of us has something special to offer the world. Each of us has our own natural gifts and talents. To be truly happy we must use our uniqueness to add value to the lives of others.

The Passion Test, which you'll take as you read this book, will help you discover your unique gift; then it's up to you to give it to those who need you.

For your freedom,

> T. Harv Eker
> CEO and president of Peak Potentials Training,
> #1 *New York Times* bestselling author of
> *Secrets of the Millionaire Mind*

THE
PASSION
TEST

"How was your trip?" Chris asked.

"It was absolutely the best and most amazing experience of my entire life," Janet replied.

"What happened?"

A perplexed expression came over Janet's face.

"I must be flippin' crazy!" she said.

You'll hear Janet's incredible story before this book is done. But first . . .

Introduction

What does it mean to live a passionate life? Exciting, fulfilling, thrilling, on fire, purposeful, turned on, motivated, entertaining, easy, fun, unstoppable. It's a life aligned with destiny.

We'd all like to feel our life is purposeful. We all want to be passionate about what we're doing, to be excited about how we spend our days, to love our lives, and to feel we're making some valuable contribution.

Yet how do you discover what it is that's your real passion? That's what this book is about.

Before we begin we have a few things to discuss with you.

1. The key to creating anything you want in your life
2. A little about who we are
3. The "inner work" this book guides you through and why it's critical to your success
4. How destiny and passion go together

So, let's get to it.

Intention—Attention—No Tension

Our friend and advisor, Bill Levacy, shared this piece of wisdom with us. We recommend you make it your mantra. It's the essence of what's required to create anything you want in your life.

Intention—Consciously stating what you choose to create in your life is the first step to manifesting it.

Attention—Give attention to what you choose to create in your life, and it will begin to show up.

No Tension—When you are open to what is appearing in this moment, you allow God's will to move through you. When you hold tightly to your concepts of how things should be, you shut off the flow of life, which in turn prevents you from enjoying the fulfillment of living your destiny.

Who We Are

If we were you, we'd be wondering, who are these people to be talking about how to live your passion?

Janet managed kitchens and hotels for thousands of people in Spain and Italy early in her career. She became the top salesperson in job after job and owned two successful businesses (one of them was rated among the top ten companies in her area). She worked for a success seminar company teaching motivational courses. She managed the telemarketing division for Books Are Fun, at the time the third-largest book buyer in the U.S. It sold to Reader's Digest for $360 million the year after her division performed at record levels.

During his career, Chris managed ten different businesses as president, general manager, or chief operating officer. In the early eighties, he rose to become president of a secondary dealer in government securities before retiring from the world for ten years to explore human consciousness and study the Vedic tradition of India.

Both of us are committed to spiritual practice. Meditation has always been the basis of our lives.

Janet followed her dreams, got sidetracked, got back to pursuing her dreams, and then got sidetracked again, a number of times. Chris went through the same kind of thing. It's not unusual for most of us to get excited and passionate and then feel we have to "be responsible," or we have a concept of what will make us happy (like getting married) and so we get off track for a while.

Some people stay off track their whole lives. In the hope that we can help you get on track, or confirm the track you're on, we have written this book.

In November 2000, Janet got a call from Mark Victor Hansen, coauthor of the phenomenally successful Chicken Soup for the Soul® series. They had become friends some years before while Janet was at Books Are Fun.

During the call, Mark said, "I'm working on a new book with Robert G. Allen, who wrote the bestselling financial book *Nothing Down*. I want you to work with us on promoting our new book."

Needless to say, Janet was thrilled. Mark explained what they had in mind. Then he asked her to put together a business plan and get it to him in three days. She describes how she felt:

> When Mark mentioned a business plan, my heart sank. This is not what I do. It was at that moment that inspiration struck.
>
> My ex-husband, Chris, and I had continued to be good friends and stayed in regular touch after our divorce. Chris has an MBA and is brilliant when it comes to things like business plans. His skills are also a perfect complement to mine, and I thought maybe we could do this project together.
>
> I called him up in California, laid out the scenario for him, and asked if he could help me put together a business plan in the next three days. He loved the idea of working with Mark and Bob, but he didn't love the idea of preparing a business plan in such a short time. He told me it would take at least three weeks and that he was way too busy with his own work to write it up.
>
> I appealed to his beautiful heart, "Couldn't you do it as my Christmas present?"
>
> Being the remarkably flexible person he is, Chris said okay, he would draft an outline of a business plan that could provide the basis for our next call with Mark and Bob.
>
> That was the beginning of an incredible partnership. Chris and I worked for a year with Mark and Bob creating the Enlightened Millionaire Program, the one-year mentoring program we designed with them based on our original business plan to help market their book.
>
> As we worked with hundreds of people in that pro-

gram, I once again discovered what it means to live life with passion.

During that year, we began teaching The Passion Test, which Janet had begun to develop for her own life in her thirties. We discovered what a profound effect it has on people. We've now given the Test to thousands of people in many different parts of the world, and it's been thrilling to hear the impact it's had on people's lives. Here are a few examples:

It wasn't until I took The Passion Test that I realized one of my five top passions was to travel to foreign countries with my two sons. Two days after taking the Test and clarifying my top passions I received an e-mail from my friends inviting me and my two sons to travel to Tonga on their boat to help film a whale expedition. To say the least, my mind was blown! Janet was right when she said, "That which you put your attention on grows stronger in your life." I recommend The Passion Test for everyone who wants to manifest *now*!

—*Dr. Jacalyn Buettner*

As an Oscar- and two-time Emmy Award–winning director I had totally lost my way. I was directing baby commercials for toy companies. Your Passion Test workshop and book brought me home to my passionate commitment to creating change through the power of films. I am now, a year later, living my dream. I am producing seven feature films and am about to direct my first feature film. I am working with amazing people and I have never been happier or more fulfilled.

—*Jeffrey Brown*

The process is incredible and so valuable for me to find my passion. For many years I have been searching for answers that have for one reason or another eluded me. I can already see that going through The Passion Test has started me on a journey to finally clarify where my passions lie. I am so excited, and my energy is just flowing as I begin the next step in the process.

—*Dee Berman*

You can find more testimonials at:
www.thepassiontest.com/testimonials

Today we support each other fully in living our passions, whether they make logical sense or not. The result has been a life that is fulfilling beyond anything we could have imagined.

We have woven the story of how Janet is fulfilling one of her passions throughout part 1 of this book. Pay attention to the lessons embedded in this story because those lessons will be critical in helping you fulfill your own destiny.

Doing the Inner Work

In our online magazine, *Healthy Wealthy nWise*, we interview famous transformational teachers every month (www.healthy wealthynwise.com/interview). Many of these teachers have commented in their interviews that most people don't want to step out of their busy world to take the necessary time to do their "inner homework." Most people are afraid if they stop "doing" then they won't be able to earn a living, take care of their family, pay the mortgage, etc.

Any great teacher will tell you that your results are not created on the gross surface "thinking" or "doing" level of life but from going deep within and tapping into the unbounded reservoir of creativity and intelligence within each of us.

In this book we will share with you some of the core knowledge necessary to live a fulfilled life on every level: personal, emotional, spiritual, physical/material. We believe that everything worth doing always has some element of fun and enjoyment in it.

So in true fun form, we have made this a participatory book. We invite you to play with us, taking an active part in the process as you read, dreaming and envisioning your passionate life as you complete the exercises you'll find here.

What Is Personal Destiny—Do You Have One?

Of course you do. We all do. Think about it. Not one person on the planet is exactly like anyone else. You are unique. You have unique gifts that no one but you can give. You have those gifts because you have a special role to play in the world that requires giving those gifts.

When you are playing that role, you are living your personal destiny. When you are aligned with your destiny, your life is joyful, delightful, exciting, and fulfilling.

Your passions are the loves of your life. They are the things that are most deeply important to you. These are the things that, when you're doing them or talking about them, light you up.

The people whom you love are associated with your passions and, in many cases, your relationship with them may *be* your passion. It's not unusual for people to list their spouse or their family or their children among their top passions. For most people, your destiny will be fulfilled as part of a team, and your family is your most fundamental team.

Passion and love are inextricably intertwined because they both arise from the heart. When you follow your passions, you will love your life.

Dr. Andrew Newberg and Mark Waldman, neuroscientists at the University of Pennsylvania's Center for Spirituality and the Mind, have extensively studied the relationships between what we believe and what we create in our world. They are coauthors of the acclaimed book *Born to Believe*.

We asked them about the idea that when you align your life with the things you love the most, you will feel an increasing sense of purposefulness, joy, and fulfillment. Here's what they said:

The brain is very happy when you're focused on what you love. The more you focus on what you truly love and desire, the volume gets turned down in those parts of the limbic system where the destructive emotions of fear, anger, depression, and anxiety are controlled. This allows you to think more clearly.

You also turn up the volume in other parts of the limbic system that generate positive emotions. When this happens, you get a release of dopamine, endorphins, and a variety of stress-reducing hormones and neurotransmitters. The more you focus on what you truly love, the healthier you are likely to be, and the more you will feel the positive effects of those stress-reducing neurochemicals in your body and mind.

You actually get kind of a double whammy. You can

have a decrease in negative emotions and an increase in positive emotions when you align yourself with what you believe is most important to you.

So, following your passions is good for your health and well-being, but how does that relate to your destiny? Your passions are not your destiny; they are the clues or keys to your purpose in life. The more passionate your life, the more closely your life is aligned with your destiny. As you read the interviews with some of the most successful people of our time in part 2 of this book, you will discover that their sense of destiny arose from the things they felt passionate about.

Destiny is a life's journey. Passions change and morph over time as one comes to know and understand oneself more deeply. As you follow your passions, you will find yourself drawn irresistibly onward until one day you wake up and find you are living a passionate life, filled with a sense of destiny.

And it begins by getting clear about your top passions, which you'll do before you finish reading this book.

Remember the mantra from the beginning of the chapter. It is the simple formula for living your personal destiny:

Intention—Attention—No Tension

Together, let's hold the intention that as you read you'll uncover your true passions and begin living the life you were put here to live.

PART
ONE

Discovering
Your Passions

THE BEGINNING
OF THE BEGINNING!

When you follow your bliss . . .
doors will open where you would not have thought
there would be doors; and where
there wouldn't be a door for anyone else.
                              —*Joseph Campbell*

"How was your trip?" Chris asked.

"It was absolutely the best and most amazing experience of
    my entire life," Janet replied.

"What happened?"

A perplexed expression came over her face.

"I must be flippin' crazy!" she said. "I got so sick I could hardly
    move out of bed for a week. I fell off a mountain and
    almost got killed. I practically froze to death in the Hi-
    malayas, got kicked by a donkey, and had to travel by
    myself in India, something I swore I'd never do."

I n spite of all this, Janet's trip to India was the best experience of her life. She met more than sixty "Saints," individuals revered for their wisdom and enlightenment. Of these, she interviewed more than forty for her upcoming documentary and book, *The Saints Speak Out*. She trekked to the source of the holy river Ganges, high in the Himalayan mountains, and she had some of the most profound insights of her life.

In a little while we'll tell you more about how Janet's passion created this life-changing trip and the remarkable experiences that came out of it, but first let's talk about the loves of *your* life.

Why are you reading this book? Maybe you want a happier, more fulfilling life. Maybe you have a feeling deep inside somewhere that your personal destiny is more than or different from what you are living right now.

We feel fortunate and grateful to have discovered how to live life immersed in our passions.

It's taken a while, over thirty years in the working world for each of us and much of that wasn't easy. We wouldn't be surprised if you know exactly what it feels like to work for weeks, months, or years doing everything you can to get yourself out of the 9 to 5, just getting by, living from paycheck to paycheck life.

Maybe you've attended seminars or watched TV programs on making money in real estate or in stocks or in your own business. Maybe you've tried to make extra money in multi-level marketing or by selling things on eBay or getting a part-time job.

Maybe you know what it's like when yet another great plan

fails, when that feeling of depression and discouragement rises up and overwhelms you, turning your insides out and making you wonder, "Is all this really worth it?"

We've been there too. We've discovered that those feelings come up when you are not aligned with your personal destiny. And it can all change in a moment, as it did for Janet.

The Light Goes On

Janet began her journey dancing under the streetlights as a child:

> When I was eight years old, I used to lie in bed at night waiting for everyone in my family to go to sleep.
>
> Then I would quietly sneak outside and enter my imaginary world. This was my favorite time of day. Underneath the corner streetlight, my world became a brightly lit stage. I became a beautiful, world-famous actress performing to thousands of ardent admirers. Into the quiet of the early morning I would sing and dance with total abandon. There on my street-corner stage I felt truly alive and free.
>
> Whenever my aunts and uncles came to visit, I always made sure Dad had me dance and sing for them. How my sister and brother hated me whenever my father gathered everyone in the living room for my Broadway show! At that moment, Mickey and Johnny would run out the back door in total embarrassment.
>
> After all, I couldn't sing on key and I didn't know how to dance. Yet my love of performing in front of any-

one far outweighed any insecurity I might feel in the talent department. Without a moment's hesitation, I would entertain anyone who came to visit.

I repeatedly begged my parents to let me attend the Pasadena Playhouse, the dramatic arts school nearby. They replied, "Sorry honey, but we just don't have the money for that sort of thing."

By the time I was ten, my dad was making more money and agreed to my long-standing request. But I felt it was no longer in the realm of possibility. Brokenhearted, I looked at my father and said, "I'd love to go to Pasadena Playhouse, but it's just too late. I'm afraid I'm already too old." I thought since I was now older than Shirley Temple when she started acting, I had blown my chance at stardom.

So in that fateful moment my fantasy world collapsed, and I entered into a world of harsh, hard realities.

Neither my brother nor sister would ever be caught playing make-believe under the early morning streetlights. It was time I grew up and saw I was just too old for that sort of thing.

And that's where I was wrong.

By the time I turned eighteen I had stopped dreaming and started living a rather uninspired version of "real life." There was never a thought about what I loved to do, hoped to do, or even wanted to do. All that was long forgotten.

When I needed a job, I just scanned the classifieds. My only questions were, how hard would I have to work and how much was the pay?

In 1981 I started working for a technical recruiting company in San Jose, California, in the heart of Silicon

Valley in its heyday, hunting for "disk drive engineers." My employer was enjoying huge success. There was a bell that rang whenever someone made a placement, and it rang many times each day.

Unfortunately, it never rang for me. I watched placement after placement being made, everyone congratulating everyone else, new cars and houses being bought, wonderful vacations being taken—while I just sat at my desk waiting for the clock to strike five. Every day I left work humiliated, angry, embarrassed, depressed, and broke. And every day I was there it got worse.

I was hired by an elite, profitable, twelve-person company for a very simple reason: almost everyone who worked there was a friend of mine. When a vacancy came up in the company, my friends all agreed, "This is the perfect job for Janet." And why not? I was known to all as a great connector, a networker, a communicator, a real dynamo of energy, someone who could get anything done.

What wasn't known about me, however, was I had absolutely no left-brain, engineer-like capabilities. It never occurred to anyone (including me) that I wouldn't be able to communicate at all with prospective disk drive engineers.

One day I happened to see a flier for a motivational course called Yes to Success. A strange awareness came over me. I knew I had to take that seminar. I had no hesitation about calling into work sick.

The course leader for the seminar was a young woman named Debra Poneman, whose key point was the importance of "finding your passion."

As I watched Debra teach the class, excitedly discussing ideas like time management and goal setting, I was less interested in what she was saying than in who she was being.

She was clearly living her passion—and it showed in her every word and gesture. Debra definitely appeared to be a truly happy person. There she was, the "ideal woman," uplifting everyone not only with her profound understanding but also with the love she radiated. At the same time, she was traveling the world, making money talking about what she loved, and doing it all so brilliantly.

Debra taught us that when we saw a person who had something we wanted, we needed to move beyond envy or resentment. Instead, we should just tell ourselves, "That's for me!"

I took that advice to heart as I watched Debra. Closing my eyes, I silently repeated my new golden mantra: "That's for me! That's for me! That's for me!"

By a stroke of wonderful good fortune, I was able to drive Debra to the airport when the course ended. As we were waiting for her plane, she stared straight into my eyes and said, "What is your dream, Janet?"

Staring right back at her, I said, "I'm glad you asked! I was just thinking today that you should either hire me or move over, because I am going to be the most successful transformational speaker on the planet."

Just then there was an announcement that the plane was ready for boarding. Without commenting at all on what I had just said, Debra gave me a hug, turned quickly, and walked off. All I could think was, "She hasn't seen the last of me!"

Once I find the direction I really want to go, I'm the kind of person who can make changes very quickly. The next day I returned to work knowing my days as an uninspired drone were about to come to an end. One thought burned in my mind: how can I convince Debra to hire me?

Finally, I came up with a plan I knew would impress her. At the end of her course, Debra passed out her schedule of appearances for the coming months, which included New York; Boston; Washington, DC; Fairfield, Iowa; and Los Angeles.

Somehow, I decided, I would get enough money, fly to every one of those places, and sit in the front row of each and every class. Whenever Debra walked into the room, she would see me sitting there and know I meant business. The only thing I needed was enough money for all the expenses involved in following Debra around.

That night I met a friend at the local Transcendental Meditation® center I used to frequent. When she casually asked what I had been doing recently, I startled her by loudly and passionately declaring I had finally discovered my purpose on this planet.

I told her about my plan to attend all of Debra's classes.

The following evening the same friend met me again at the TM center. As we were getting up from meditation, she opened her purse, showered ten crisp one hundred–dollar bills on my head, and laughingly said, "Merry Christmas!" I just sat there with my mouth open. As tears came to my eyes, I thanked her for believing in me and promised that very soon I would repay her incredible generosity.

I followed my plan, going from city to city to each of Debra's seminars. Finally, in Los Angeles, at the last seminar on her schedule, she came up to me and said,

"Okay, if I can't get rid of you, then I better make use of you. You're hired!"

Needless to say, this was a thrilling moment. I was on my way to my dream. However, as I sat through Debra's seminars, time after time, something much more important happened: the birth of The Passion Test.

2

THE PASSION TEST
IS BORN

I am here for a purpose and that purpose
is to grow into a mountain,
not to shrink to a grain of sand.
Henceforth will I apply ALL my efforts
to become the highest mountain of all
and I will strain my potential
until it cries for mercy.

—*Og Mandino*

Passion is a very personal experience. When you begin to do what you love, what you are truly passionate about, your life will be irresistibly pulled in directions you can't even begin to imagine.

Through the course of part 1 of this book we'll share with you the astonishing story of the miracles that appeared in Janet's life as a result of gaining clarity about the greatest loves in her life: her passions.

Often we get bogged down in the "hows": How will I find the money? How will I find the time? How will I learn this or that skill? But as you'll see, it's not the "how" that is important for you to know; it's the "what." And helping you get clear on the "what"—what your passions truly are—is what this book is all about.

As the story of Janet's trip to India unfolds, you'll see how money appeared from nowhere and how rather than running after her desires, her desires came to her. We'll share the serendipitous events that she could never have predicted and how the surface inconveniences or discomforts that inevitably appear along the path of passion become irrelevant when one is aligned with destiny.

With all that to look forward to, let's return now to Janet's story of the birth of The Passion Test.

> On the second day of her seminar, Debra mentioned a survey of one hundred of the most influential, financially successful individuals in the United States. The survey found that all of these supersuccessful, powerful people had one thing in common.
>
> "Can any of you guess what that one thing is?" she asked.
>
> We each blurted out what we thought might be the magic answer, but Debra just kept shaking her head.
>
> "What could that one thing be?" I thought.
>
> Finally, after what seemed like forever, Debra said, "The survey found that these powerful, successful people had totally fulfilled the five things that they felt were most necessary for their ideal life."
>
> With that one sentence, my life was changed forever.
>
> In other words, the light went on.
>
> Actually, it was more like fireworks!
>
> Debra continued talking about the importance of knowing what it is you want to be, do, and have; how

> once you set goals, you too can become powerful and successful. It was so easy.
>
> As Debra segued into talking about how to dress for success, I was still in my own world, thinking about the survey. "Clearly what one has to do is determine one's own most important aspirations," I thought.

When she got home, Janet sat down and made a list of fifteen of the things she would love to do, be, or have in her life. She then sorted out her top five.

1. I am a brilliant, successful transformational speaker uplifting humanity all over the world
2. I travel the world first class
3. I am treated like a queen wherever I go
4. I give and receive love in every part of my life
5. I work with an enlightened team

The simple and unique process she used to sort them out is what is now known as The Passion Test.

We'll introduce you to The Passion Test in a moment, but first, why is it so important to do what you love? A friend shared a true story that illustrates the importance of doing what you enjoy perfectly. It went like this:

A young girl who collected autographs of famous people was at the airport waiting to board her plane when she saw a crowd of people standing around a small man in a white robe.

She knew this man had to be someone well known because of the large crowd around him. She went up to one of the people standing nearby and asked who the man was. She was told, "That's Maharishi Mahesh Yogi, a great Saint from the Himalayas."

The girl excitedly ran up to Maharishi and immediately asked for his autograph. Maharishi took her pen and paper, looked her straight in the eyes, and said, "I will give you something much more important than my autograph." And on the piece of paper he wrote one word.

Enjoy

What was the message Maharishi was conveying? The whole purpose of life is to enjoy. When you are not enjoying you are out of the flow of life. You are missing your purpose.

Again, what's so important about enjoying what you are doing? Think about all the greatest people on the planet, past and present. Every one of them, without exception, loved what they did or are now doing. Every single one of them. Their lives may not have been easy, they certainly faced challenges, and yet, they *loved* what they were doing.

Now think about the people you know who are truly happy. Don't they love what they are doing in their lives? Maybe there are some parts of their lives that are challenging, but when it comes down to it, they love their lives, how they spend their days, and who they spend their lives with, don't they?

For us, it is obvious. To have absolute success in any area, the most important prerequisite must be that you have a passion for doing it.

Do passion and enjoyment go hand in hand? Absolutely! Passion is the inner fire that propels you forward through the combination of love for what you're doing and the inner sense of purpose that comes from connecting to one's deepest passions. Enjoyment arises from this combination of love and purposefulness.

By helping you clarify what it is you love most, what is most important to you, The Passion Test gives you the means to align your life with what you most enjoy.

The Passion Test is also powerful because it's a system.

Webster's dictionary defines the word *system* like this:

sys·tem

1. a regularly interacting or interdependent group of items forming a unified whole . . .
2. an organized set of doctrines, ideas, or principles usually intended to explain the arrangement or working of a systematic whole . . .
3. a: an organized or established procedure <the touch *system* of typing> b: a manner of classifying, symbolizing, or schematizing <a taxonomic *system*> <the decimal *system*>
4. harmonious arrangement or pattern : ORDER <bring *system* out of confusion—Ellen Glasgow>

A system provides order, saves time, requires less energy, and costs less. It is an organized, established procedure that produces results. An easy way to remember the value of a system is the acronym Robert Allen and Mark Victor Hansen coined for system in their book *The One Minute Millionaire*. SYSTEM = Save Yourself Time, Energy, and Money.

The Passion Test is a system that will help you discover your mission in life. What is your purpose? What is your destiny? What is the work that feels like play no matter how many hours you put into it?

The Passion Test is very simple, but don't let that fool you. Its results can be profound. It will give you an easy, fun way to prioritize the things that truly mean the most to you. It will help you eliminate the things that are distractions right now.

The Passion Test requires you to face your inner life and bring it out to the surface, so you can examine it and clarify what is really most important to you. It is the magical key that will unlock those forgotten dreams that wait patiently in your heart for the day when you are finally ready to say, "I am here to make a difference and the time is *now*!"

3

TAKING THE PASSION TEST

God has given each of us
our "marching orders."
Our purpose here on Earth
is to find those orders and carry them out.
Those orders acknowledge our special gifts.
—*Søren Kierkegaard*

It was 2003. We had completed our project with Mark Victor Hansen and Robert Allen. While working with them we developed incredible contacts and formed Enlightened Alliances, enjoying some great successes. Liz and Ric Thompson, members of the Enlightened Millionaire Program, had approached us with the idea of partnering with them in running their online magazine, *Healthy Wealthy nWise*, which we now do together.

Janet felt it was time to once again clarify her passions. She had taken The Passion Test many times before, but this time was different. Something was stirring inside that she knew was going to have a profound effect on her life.

As she made her list of the things that are most deeply important to her, what she will be, do, or have when her life is ideal, she realized she had more clarity about these things than ever before.

One item on the list jumped out: "Spending time with the enlightened." It was as if this short phrase was a spark that ignited an insatiable fire inside her.

Even as she felt deeply drawn to this idea, she thought, "How in the world will I ever do that?" After all, those who are most revered for their wisdom and enlightenment are either surrounded by huge organizations with lots of people protecting them or hidden away in caves high in the Himalayas or in dense forests.

She knew she wanted to begin by traveling to India, because she had already met some enlightened masters there, but beyond that she had no clue how her passion could possibly be fulfilled.

Before we tell you how Janet's passion for spending time with the enlightened was realized, and continues to be, you need to take The Passion Test yourself. Just remember, for now, you don't need to figure out *how* any of the passions you put on your list will be realized. We'll help you with that once you get them down on paper.

In giving people The Passion Test, we have found the biggest challenge for most people is getting out of their own way. When most people first take The Passion Test, they start to write down a passion, but if they can't immediately see how they can practically manifest it, they erase it (especially the really big ones!) and put something down that they can easily put their arms around. In other words, they play it "safe."

For example, maybe you yearn to be a world-renowned

concert pianist. Now, from your present life situation that may seem totally unrealistic. So instead of listing your passion as being a concert pianist, you play it safe and write, "playing the piano."

We can hear your thoughts now: "But I don't have any idea how I'm going to become a world-renowned concert pianist." Trust us. It doesn't matter. Write it down.

Dr. Andrew Newberg and Mark Waldman, the neuroscientists at the University of Pennsylvania's Center for Spirituality and the Mind whom we mentioned in the introduction, had this to say about thinking big:

When we focus on the big questions, the really *big* questions, we are challenging our brains to think outside the box, and this causes the structure of our neurons to change, particularly in our frontal lobes, that part of the brain that controls logic, reason, language, consciousness, and compassion.

New axons grow, reaching out to new dendrites to communicate in ways that our brains have never done before. When contemplating the *big* questions, we use our frontal lobes to alter the function of other parts of our brain.

So, don't be afraid to think *big*. Janet didn't have a clue how she'd be able to spend time with enlightened masters when she wrote down, "spend time with the enlightened." Yet you'll see as her story unfolds, the result was much better than anything she could have ever dreamed up.

Once your intention is clear, attention is the next step. If you think your passion is becoming a multimillionaire and you don't have any inclination to put your attention on making money and creating wealth, then your mind is playing games with you. It is telling you this is your passion when in fact it just wants to be safe from bills, responsibilities, and discomfort. Such mind games never lead to fulfillment.

Passions arise from the heart. When you are truly passionate about something, you don't have to try hard to put attention on it. When challenges arise, they can't deter you. They may slow you down for a little while, but they can't stop you.

Let's come back to this idea of "playing it safe." Have you ever noticed people who play it safe aren't at all as enthusiastic, energetic, full of passion, on fire, and excited about their lives as your friends who dance around on the edge and totally go for their dreams?

Think about someone you know who always chooses the safe route. When looking for a job, they'll take the lower salary with health insurance, retirement benefits, and paid vacation, with an established company, rather than take the risks in a start-up that may pay more, have a more family-like atmosphere, and offer stock options.

Those people don't hike too close to the edge of the cliff, don't jump off the high dive, don't travel to areas where they might encounter some awful disease. They don't live where they'd love to because it costs too much, don't fly in small planes, don't drive at high speeds, don't sail across the ocean, don't do anything that might be dangerous, risky, or scary.

Are those the kind of people you want to be like?

On the other hand, what's it like to be someone who goes for the gusto in every moment? What does it feel like to be someone who is doing whatever it takes to live their dream; who is willing to face any challenge, jump through any hoops, go anywhere they have to, in pursuit of their heart's dearest desires?

Don't get us wrong here, we're not going to tell you to jump off the mountain until you're ready, but we do want to impress upon you the importance of thinking of your *ideal* life, not your *possible* life.

There is a secret to sorting out the "how" of your dreams, which we will share with you a little later. This secret is revealed in the story of Janet's trip to India, and that trip would never have happened if she hadn't first given herself permission to be open to all possibilities as she clarified the "what."

So right now, please trust us. Don't censor your Passion Test.

To make sure you are going to set free those *big passions* that so far have yet to come out, Janet will share with you, as an example, the passions list of a friend who has no problem thinking big.

> A couple of years ago Chris and I were speaking at T. Harv Eker's Wealth and Wisdom seminar in Vancouver. My great friend and associate Jack Canfield of Chicken Soup for the Soul fame was also a featured presenter.
>
> At the time I was writing my e-book, *The Passion Test: Discovering Your Personal Secrets to Living a Life on Fire.* I wanted to take Jack through the Test so I could use it in my book.
>
> I rang Jack up in his hotel room on the morning he was leaving for California and asked if I could meet with him before he left to give him The Passion Test. Jack said the timing just wouldn't work because he was on his way to the airport and his taxi was waiting.
>
> "No problem," I said. "Can I come along and give you the Test on the way?"

> I can still hear Jack chuckling through the phone as he said, "You're a crazy redhead! Okay—meet you downstairs."
>
> On the way to the airport I explained to Jack how The Passion Test worked, and in about one minute he had shot out fifteen of his greatest passions.
>
> Talk about knowing who you are and what you love!
>
> I wasn't surprised. With over 100 million Chicken Soup for the Soul books sold worldwide, obviously the guy knows where he wants to go, and he definitely doesn't have a problem thinking big enough.

Here's Jack's initial list of passions.

1. Being of service to massive numbers of people
2. Having an international impact
3. Enjoying celebrity status
4. Being part of a dynamic team
5. Having a leadership role
6. Helping people live their vision
7. Speaking to large groups
8. Having an impact through television
9. Being a multimillionaire
10. Having world-class quarters and support team
11. Having lots of free time
12. Studying with spiritual masters regularly
13. Being part of a spiritual leaders network
14. Creating a core group of ongoing trainers who feel identified with my organization
15. Having fun, fun, fun!

Here's what Jack's Test results looked like after I walked him through The Passion Test process.

1. Helping people live their vision
2. Being part of a dynamic team
3. Being of service to massive numbers of people
4. Having an international impact
5. Creating a core group of ongoing trainers who feel identified with my organization

> Just like the very successful people in the study that inspired The Passion Test, after going through the Test, Jack told me all five of his passions were already completely actualized in his life. But one thing surprised Jack. Being part of a spiritual leaders network was #6 after The Passion Test process. Although it was very important to him, this passion was nowhere in Jack's life yet. As we said good-bye, he told me he was going to get started on that one right away.

Today, Chris and I are pleased to be founding members of Jack's Transformational Leadership Council, a growing group of over one hundred speakers, authors, and trainers from around the world, formed by Jack. He created this group not long after he took The Passion Test and saw that being part of such a network was important to him. Okay, I'm obviously proud of my little test for being part of the birthing of one of Jack's dreams. Enough said.

Now back to Jack's Test. Notice anything about it? Almost every one of his passions is a pretty darn big one. Was Jack concerned when I gave him the Test whether he could fulfill his passions? Absolutely not. The next principle I am now going to offer you was already encoded in Jack's DNA way before he took the Test.

When you are clear,
what you want will show up in your life,
and only to the extent that you are clear.

The opposite of this is also true: fuzzy desires give fuzzy results. The vast majority of this book is dedicated to helping you achieve greater clarity. We will give you a number of tools to help you clarify your passions as we continue.

Now let's review the guidelines for doing your own Test.

Passion Test Guidelines

The first part of The Passion Test is to make a list of your passions; i.e., those things that you love most, are most important to you, and are most critical to your happiness and well-being.

As you prepare your initial list of passions, play full-out—no holding back. Write down at least ten and as many as fifteen or more things that you absolutely love.

What you're after here are your passions, not your goals. Passions are how you live your life. Goals are the things you choose to create in your life. For example, one of Jack's passions is "being a multimillionaire." Even if Jack wasn't already a multimillionaire, his passion would be stated as "being a multimillionaire." However, he may have a goal to earn $2 million in the next year.

What's the difference? A passion is how you choose to live your life. Jack chooses to live life as a multimillionaire. A goal is something you aim to achieve. The goal could be stated as "to earn $2 million within the next year."

When your passions are clear you can create goals that are aligned with your passions and begin to create the life you choose to live. Both passions and goals are valuable, and the first step is getting clear on your passions. Think about what you will do, be, and have when your life is ideal.

As Jack did with his list, begin each passion with a verb that expresses how you are living life when your life is ideal.

Here are examples of passions some of our students have expressed.

- Living in a beautiful home in which I feel completely at peace
- Writing successful mystery novels
- Working in a nurturing environment with lots of plants and light
- Enjoying perfect health with lots of energy, stamina, and vitality
- Having fun with everything I do
- Spending lots of quality time with my family
- Enjoying great sex on a regular basis
- Working with a supportive team of people who share my values

Okay, those are all good and fine. What if your passions are altruistic, like having a peaceful world or eliminating poverty on earth or eradicating disease?

Remember, passions are how you live your life. Goals are things that you achieve.

Living a life of peace could be a passion. Creating peace in the world is a goal. Living life in abundance could be a passion. Eliminating poverty on earth is a goal.

Now, could someone have a passion for eliminating poverty on earth or ending world hunger? Absolutely. Lynne Twist, a member of the Transformational Leadership Council, is a great example. Lynne spent many years as a fund-raiser and leader of the Hunger Project, an international organization that has had a huge impact in eliminating world hunger. Lynne's passion was *working* to end world hunger. The *goal* of the Hunger Project is to end world hunger.

Do you get the difference? Passions are about process. Goals are about outcomes.

As you think about your list of passions, here are some ideas to help get you going:

Loves and Talents: Clues to Your Unique Gifts

What do you love to do? What kind of environment do you love to be in? What kind of people do you love to be around? What excites you, turns you on, gets you charged up? The answers to these questions all provide clues to your purpose.

Here's another set of clues: What are you good at? What do people compliment you on? What do you seem to do better than most others? What are your unique skills and talents?

You most likely enjoy doing the things you're good at, so loves and talents often go together.

Beware the Mind

If that's all there is to it, why do so many people fail to fulfill their life's purpose? Because your mind tends to trick you. The mind is like a monkey, jumping here and there and everywhere.

First it's running toward something enticing; then it's running away from something scary. Your mind will even try to convince you, in the name of safety and security, that your life's purpose is something less than it really is.

For example, many people tell us their passion is to make lots of money. But some of them have no attraction to things that have to do with money, making money, or creating more money. These people may have a passion for service or a passion for their family or a passion for being in nature. There is nothing about making money, per se, that attracts them, turns them on, or gets them excited. When we talk to them, what we discover is they don't care so much about having lots of money as they do about feeling the freedom to do the things they love.

It's not necessary to have lots of money to have that freedom. For example, Mother Teresa had complete freedom to do the things she loved, yet she never had lots of money. The same is true of Mahatma Gandhi and Martin Luther King.

On the other hand, we've met some people (Harv Eker comes to mind) who have a burning passion to make lots of money combined with a passion to help lots of people at the same time. There is nothing that can stop those people from making money. They are so focused on making lots of money that there's no way it can't show up.

Be open to receiving support from wherever it may come and you will find fulfillment growing in your life. If the security and freedom money provides are very important to you, then they will show up.

Making money and creating wealth are learned skills for most people. To have money and wealth requires either investing the time, energy, and money to learn those skills or surrounding yourself with people who have them.

A Few Other Guidelines Worth Mentioning

As you make your list, keep the following in mind.

- Don't consult with anyone. This is about the things that light *your* fire. Go deep inside and connect with the things that are truly most important to you.
- Don't take the Test as a couple. Do the process on your own. Later, if you choose, you can share your passions with your spouse or partner. If you really, really want to do it together, then each of you prepare your own initial list and afterward take each other through The Passion Test process. If you do this, *don't* try to influence your partner's choices. It's their Test. If you don't like their choices, then think about whether you can love them enough to want for them what they want for themselves.
- We recommend you take the Test in one sitting. It should only take twenty to thirty minutes unless you

aren't at all clear about what things are most important to you; then it could take a little longer.

- If possible, take the Test in a quiet environment, without distractions. This is a process of going deep within
to those things that mean most to you in your life. You
won't find them when you're stirred up or having to
pay attention to other things.

- Write short, clear sentences. Avoid combining several
passions in one, such as "I am enjoying my ideal relationship, traveling the world first class, and living in a
beautiful home overlooking the ocean." Break each
passion down and list it separately; i.e.: "I am enjoying
my ideal relationship." "I am traveling the world first
class." "I am living in a beautiful home overlooking the
ocean."

The Passion Test is a tool to help you understand the key
success elements for *you* to live a happy, fulfilled life. It is very
personal. Your five will not be exactly the same as anyone
else's. Just remember, happy, successful people have all five of
their top passions present in their life. The Passion Test will
help you identify your top five and put you on the road to a
fulfilling life.

Passion Test Instructions

Step One

First, make a list of at least ten of the most important things
you can think of that would give you a life of joy, passion, and

fulfillment. Begin each one with a verb relating to being, doing, or having, which completes the sentence:

When my life is ideal, I am _____.

Close your eyes and picture your ideal life. What are you doing? Who are you with? Where are you? How do you feel?

Now make your list and know that this is just your first list. If you follow our advice and take the Test every six months, you'll be doing this many, many times over the coming years, getting clearer every time. Don't censor. You don't need to know the how, just the what.

Make your list now—at least ten (and as many as you want):

1. _____
2. _____
3. _____
4. _____
5. _____
6. _____
7. _____
8. _____
9. _____
10. _____
11. _____
12. _____
13. _____
14. _____
15. _____

Let your list sit for a while. Come back to it in a few hours or tomorrow.

Step Two

When you return to your list, use the following steps to compare the items and identify which are the most important to you.

a. If you had to choose between having the first passion on your list and the second, which would you choose? Keep in mind that in making your choice you are not losing anything. Comparing the two items as if you could only have one of them is necessary to help you get in touch with what is most deeply important to you. In real life you can certainly have both, and by the time you finish all the exercises in this book you will see that everything is included.

b. Continue comparing the one you choose with the next number until you go through the whole list, and then label the one you chose as number 1. For example, if you compared the first item on the list to the second, and you chose the second, then you would next compare the second item to the third. If you again chose the second item, then you'd compare the second item to the fourth and so on, always comparing your choice to the next item on the list.

Keep in mind that if you compare 1 to 2 and choose 1, then compare 1 to 3 and choose 3, you don't need to go back and compare 3 to 2. You already know that 1 is more important than 2, and if 3 is more important than 1 then 3 is also, by definition, more important than 2.

c. Start again, and compare each item that remains (don't include the ones you've already chosen), always keeping the one that's more important. When you get to the end of the list, label the remaining choice 2. Go through the list again and label the remaining choice 3, and so on until you identify your five most important passions.

d. If you get stuck and can't decide which item is more important, then ask yourself, "If I could be, do, or have 1 and *never* do 2, or if I could be 2 and *never* be, do, or have 1, which one matters most to me?" By stating your choice clearly as an either/or choice, you will gain the deepest insights. Avoid saying, "They are both equally important to me." In our experience, this is just a lack of clarity. Go deeper.

e. Most people find that their first impulse is the most accurate. Passion arises from the heart, and your heart's impulse is more likely to be closer to the truth than your mind's analysis.

f. Be honest. Don't worry if your choices aren't what others think they should be. You don't have to show this list to anyone else. This is about what lights your fire, right now. The more closely aligned you are with what you truly love, the happier and more fulfilled you will be. The happier you are, the more attractive you will be to those you love and cherish. As a great teacher once said, "Happiness radiates like the fragrance from a flower and draws all good things toward you."

g. Avoid the temptation to get to an item on your list that seems really important and to say, "Oh, that's number one, so I don't need to go through the rest of the list." We can't begin to tell you how many times we have taken people through the Test, had them say, "I know without going through this process what my number one passion is," only to discover that things changed as they went through the complete list. So go through the comparison process with every item on your list for all five of your top passions.

h. Don't be surprised if the choices you make change each time you go through the list. When you are simple and innocent, going through the process without holding on to any agenda, your mind and heart will go deeper each time you go through the list. As this happens, it's not unusual for your choices to change as you continue. If you want to get an idea of what some others have written for their Passion Test, go to: http://www.thepassiontest.com/results.

Dr. Andrew Newberg and Mark Waldman, the neuroscientists who authored *Born to Believe,* gave some advice worth keeping in mind as you take The Passion Test:

When we introduce a new idea into the brain, there's going to be an interesting confusion and cognitive dissonance at first. It may feel uncomfortable. The brain doesn't necessarily like new ideas, especially if they conflict with older beliefs that you've embraced in the past. So, if you spent years nurturing low self-esteem and you suddenly decide to introduce the notion that you are truly a wonderful person, two neural circuits must compete: the old memory and the new idea.

When something new comes in, the brain goes into

an alert state. The amygdala is saying, "Wake up, pay attention, there's something different happening in my body or the world. Is it safe or dangerous?" People will need to sift through this period of discomfort as they realign their lives with their passions.

One very interesting neurological finding suggests that you can only hold about seven chunks of information in consciousness at one time. When more information comes in, the brain filters out those elements it deems unimportant. So, if you try to hold on to too many ideas, desires, or goals at one time, the brain says, "This is too much. I can only keep so much in focus."

In our opinion, from a neuroscientific point of view, The Passion Test process is very important because it will help keep you focused on those things that matter most to you. The clearer you become about what you truly love and desire, the stronger your conscious intention becomes, and this helps the rest of your brain respond in an organized way.

What was that mantra we shared with you earlier?

**When you are clear,
what you want will show up in your life,
and only to the extent that you are clear.**

Magic happens when you are clear. You will find yourself saying, "That was the best experience of my life!" And so it was for Janet as she began thinking about how she would manifest her love for "spending time with the enlightened."

CREATING YOUR
PASSIONATE LIFE

The person born with a talent
they are meant to use will find
their greatest happiness in using it.
—*Johann Wolfgang von Goethe*

"Okay ... I can do this. After all, I've been networking most of my life, and finding Saints to interview can't be any harder than finding a movie star or any other famous person.

"Hmm ... let me see. Why would they want to see me anyway?"

These and similar thoughts went racing through my head as I looked at this new, number one passion in my life. "Where do I start, with something so far outside of 'normal' life?" I wondered.

Have you ever been totally perplexed by a problem, challenge, or situation? The more you think about it, the more perplexing it becomes. Sometimes the best thing you can do is just forget about it for a while, and that's what I did.

Then one day a friend called. "Janet, there is this wonderful Saint from India coming to Chicago. You should interview him for your magazine."

It was an *aha* moment.

"That's it! If I write articles for our magazine about enlightened Saints, I could turn them into a book, and the Saints might be willing to spend time with me in order to get their message out. Now that would be fun!" I thought.

A plan began to emerge. "I'll contact my friends who have lived in India or traveled there frequently, find out who in India is most revered for their wisdom and knowledge, and see if these Saints will let me interview them." It was a good plan; I just needed a little guidance.

I got on the phone to Bill Levacy, an expert in Vedic astrology, to get his advice on the trip. He encouraged me to go, "Just be sure to take a video camera with you to record your interviews. It doesn't have to be anything fancy, just have the camera there and record your sessions with the Saints."

Another epiphany.

"I'll create a documentary! What more important thing can I do than to bring people throughout the world the insights of the wise regarding what we need to do about the current world situation?" I was on cloud nine, floating in the vision of sitting at the feet of the wisest teachers in the world, when all of a sudden, I came crashing back to the ground.

"This could cost a lot of money, especially the way I

like to travel! All of my money is tied up in our business. How will I ever pay for this trip, not to mention the equipment I'll need?" Reality hit hard.

W e'll tell you how hundreds of thousands of dollars came to Janet in the next few months, but first we need to help you score your passions and create your Passion Cards.

You've identified the five that you love, the things that are most important to you in your life right now. Will these change? Absolutely.

We take The Passion Test every six months because we know that as our experience of life grows we come to know ourselves ever more deeply. You may get married, have children; new opportunities will show up, you will make new discoveries. Life is constantly evolving, and with that evolution comes greater clarity about what is most important.

For example, when Chris first started using The Passion Test, he was a senior executive for a successful consulting and training company. One of his top five passions was "Determining my own hours."

Today that passion is nowhere to be found on Chris's list. The fact that he has complete control over his own hours might have something to do with that.

However, when you look at his current list, you see that his number two passion is "Having fun with everything I do." When you talk to him about what this means to him, part of having fun for Chris is having the freedom to do what he wants, when he wants.

The way in which Chris expresses his passion today is different from what it was years ago. He's discovered that "Determining my own hours" is just part of a deeper passion, which is "Having fun with everything I do."

The deeper you know yourself, the more completely you are able to align with your personal destiny.

For right now, you've created the only list that really matters: the list of your passions as you know them now. It's time for another mantra:

**What you put your attention on
grows stronger in your life.**

From a physiological perspective, here's what Dr. Andrew Newberg and Mark Waldman, the neuroscientists from the University of Pennsylvania's Center for Spirituality and the Mind, say happens in our brains:

The more you give attention to a particular belief, the stronger those neural connections in your brain become. When you focus on the positive aspects of your life, those neural pathways become stronger, and that becomes increasingly true for you. Putting attention on negative beliefs about yourself or your environment will similarly result in stronger neural connections, and those beliefs, in turn, will become more and more true for you. It literally becomes your inner reality, and that, of course, is going to influence the outer reality as well.

You are constantly creating your life. We all are. We create our life out of the things to which we give our attention. And you attract into your life more of what you put attention on.

If your attention is on all the things you don't have, all the problems in your life, all the bad things that are happening to you, then you are creating more of that.

If you want more problems, more challenges, more unhappiness, then give attention to those things. If you want more passion, fulfillment, and joy in your life, then give your attention to the things that create those feelings.

Out of fear, people focus on what they don't want. They're afraid they won't have enough money or they'll get sick or there will be a disaster. One of our favorite sayings is, "Fear is vividly imagining exactly what you don't want to happen, happening."

Focusing on what you don't want is a habit. Whenever you notice that you are focusing on something in a negative way, just say "cancel" and replace that thought with something you choose to create.

Let's try it right now. Put down the book and close your eyes. Imagine something you fear could happen to you. As soon as it appears, say "cancel" and shift your attention to the opposite. Isn't that just as likely? You can shift your life just that easily.

Because of those neural pathways Mark Waldman and Andrew Newberg were talking about, these fearful thoughts may continue to come up for a while. Just keep canceling those thoughts and replacing them with their opposites. With a little time new neural pathways will be created and your experience will change.

Your Passion Score

Would you like a simple way to discover where you've been putting your attention up until now? Okay, you've twisted our arms, here it is.

Go through the top five passions you identified from your Passion Test and rate each one on a scale of 0 to 10. Zero means you're not living that passion in your life at all. Ten means you are fully living it.

Go ahead and do that now.

Did you notice any significant differences in the scores? Most people do.

The passions that have low scores are the ones you haven't given as much attention to. The passions with high scores have received a lot of your attention.

Could it happen that you think you've been giving a lot of attention to something and the score is still low? Possibly. If you think that's the case, look carefully at where your attention has really been.

For example, suppose one of your passions is to own a multimillion-dollar business. You've been working on your business for several years, and it's still just getting by, barely supporting you. Doesn't sound like a 10 does it?

So you say, "I've been putting lots of attention on my business, and it's still just getting by."

Go back and think about where you have really been putting your attention. Has your attention been fully focused on the value you are providing to your customers? Have you been fully focused on treating each customer with honor and respect so they go away grateful for having the chance to do business with you? Have you been putting your attention on all the successes and profits that are flowing to you?

Or has your attention gone to all the bills you have to pay? Or how unreasonable some customers are? Or how little you have left over at the end of each month? Or how deeply in debt you are?

When we say, "What you put your attention on grows stronger in your life," we don't mean that putting attention on something in some generalized, fuzzy, nonspecific way will make the things you want appear in your life. We mean what you give attention to, every moment of every day, day in and day out, determines what is created in your life.

If your attention is on all the things you can't have and can't do, then you won't have them and you won't be able to do them. If your attention is on the benefits, blessings, and good fortune flowing into your life, then you will find more and more of those things showing up.

If you are really honest with yourself, you will discover that where you put your attention is creating the results you are experiencing in your life.

The great news is that where you place your attention is primarily a habit. Given about twenty-one days of consistently applying a new behavior, you can change any habit. All that is required is the will to make the change.

If you find you're having trouble changing the habit of thinking about the problems, difficulties, or challenges in your life, here's another useful technique.

Get a rubber band and put it on your wrist. Wear it seven days a week, twenty-four hours a day, for at least thirty days.

Every time you have a thought that you know is not creating what you want in your life, pull the rubber band away from your wrist and let it snap back against your skin. Ouch!

Yes, you'll feel it. And that tactile reminder will help train your mind that these types of thoughts don't serve you.

Do this for a month and you'll find you have taken a big step in breaking the habit of putting your attention on things that create unhappiness and failure in your life.

Your Passion Cards

Since you're now committed to keeping your attention on your passions, we'll share a proven method for creating whatever you want in your life.

Some years ago when we were partners with Mark Victor Hansen and Robert Allen, Janet was in Phoenix, Arizona, at an event where the well-known motivational speaker Bob Proctor was presenting. She tells the story:

> One of the first things Bob said when he got up to speak was, "Do you know how easy it is to be wealthy? I currently have more than four hundred streams of income—and it's all because of this little card."
>
> He reached into his coat, withdrew a file card, and showed it to the group. It said, "I am thankful and happy for the following . . ." and it listed his five goals in order of priority.
>
> Bob explained that the mind is like a computer: Whatever you input into the mind has to get printed out or show up in your universe sooner or later. Most

people spend their time putting their attention on what they lack instead of what they choose to create, and so they get more lack.

Holding up his small card, Bob had an infectious smile on his face when he said to the group, "One of the most important parts of my day is spent looking at this little card."

He explained that he put file cards with his goals in strategic places so he could easily glance at them from time to time during the day. As soon as one goal was fulfilled, he replaced it with a new one.

"It's that easy," he said.

Now it's time to put Bob's advice into practice as applied to your passions.

Get a number of three-by-five-inch cards. Write your passions on each card like this:

MY PASSION TEST

Date: ___/___/___

When my life is ideal I am:

1. _____
2. _____
3. _____
4. _____
5. _____

This or something better!

What was that last little line at the bottom?

"This or something better!" In our experience, the universe almost always has a better plan in mind for us than what we can think up, as long as we're open to receive it. Soon you'll see an example of how true that is, when we tell you how Janet's passion for being with the enlightened got fulfilled.

Here's a sure-fire rule that will guarantee you a passionate life:

**Whenever you are faced
with a choice, a decision, or an opportunity,
choose in favor of your passions.**

In order to choose in favor of your passions, you have to remember what they are, at the time you are making a decision. How do you do that? By having them where you will see them when choices arise. Put the three-by-five cards somewhere you will see them several times a day. What are good places?

- Your bathroom mirror, so you see your passions first thing in the morning
- By your computer, so you see your passions while you're writing e-mail
- In your purse or wallet, so you can refer to them at any time during the day
- On the dashboard of your car, so you see them when you are going places
- On the refrigerator, so you see them while preparing meals or getting snacks

The purpose of posting these cards is to keep your attention easily on your passions. You don't have to study the cards. You don't have to concentrate on them. You don't have to create plans to figure out how to live them (although there is nothing wrong with that when you feel inspired). The critical thing is to choose in favor of your passions whenever you are faced with a choice, a decision, or an opportunity.

What you need to do is read through your passions several times a day so they become deeply ingrained. So deeply ingrained that whenever you are faced with a decision you can ask yourself, is this going to help me be more aligned with my passions or less aligned?

Writing out your Passion Cards and posting them is your most important first step in creating your passionate life. So, go post your cards now and be open to receive the unexpected in your life.

CREATING YOUR MARKERS

We are at our very best, and we are happiest,
when we are fully engaged in work we enjoy,
on the journey toward the goal we've established for ourselves.
It gives meaning to our time off and comfort to our sleep.
It makes everything else in life so wonderful, so worthwhile.

—*Earl Nightingale*

Creating Markers for your passions gives you mile-
stones, or guideposts, so you know when you are on
the path of living your passions. We'll show you how
to create your Markers in a minute.

Staying open to what is appearing in your life and adjust-
ing your passions appropriately to changing situations and
circumstances is critical to following the path of your destiny.
You can never know what will show up, or how it will turn
out, as Janet discovered.

"Why are you packing two big suitcases when you are
only going to Santa Barbara for four days?" Chris asked.

"I know. Pretty weird, huh?" I replied. "I'm just too tired to think about what I need, and it really doesn't matter. It's always nice to have choices. You never know what could come up. You know me, I like to be ready for anything."

I was on my way to Santa Barbara, California, to meet Jack Canfield and other well-known writers and speakers for the first meeting of the Transformational Leadership Council.

While there I spent a few days with my girlfriend Christian. When we went out to lunch, I shared my plan to create a documentary.

"I've never used a video camera in my life," I told Christian. "I'd love to hire a professional to come along and do the filming for me."

"Do you know anyone?" she asked.

"There is one woman I really like, named Juliann, whom I met several years ago. I think she has done production or editing in Hollywood for some time, but I haven't talked with her in a couple of years."

Brrrrrng, brrrrrrng. It was my cell phone.

"Hello?"

"Hi, Janet? This is Juliann Janus."

I almost dropped my cell phone in my salad! After not being in contact for several years, what were the chances that Juliann would call me at the exact moment I was telling Christian about her?

"How did you find me?" I asked.

"Right now I'm driving down the freeway in San Diego with my friend Stephanie. We're on our way to the Prince concert and were just talking about what's going on in our lives. Stephanie tells me she is going to India and when I asked her who with, she said, 'Janet Attwood.'

"I told her, 'Janet Attwood—I love Janet Attwood. Let's call her right now!'"

In thinking about ways to finance my trip to India, I planned a tour for women to some of the famous sacred spots in that spiritual land. It turned out that one of the women who had signed up was a friend of Juliann's.

I had to find out if this was the answer to my prayers, so I asked, "Look Juliann, I don't know what you are up to, but is there any chance you'd want to go to India with me and film Saints?"

As it turned out, Juliann was completely bored with her present work situation and going to India sounded like just the adventure she felt she needed. I told her I would call her once I got home and we would continue making the necessary plans.

On the day I was to leave Santa Barbara I woke up in the morning with the clearest intuition that I wasn't supposed to leave California yet. I called my brother, John, in San Diego to tell him I was coming to spend time with him and our stepmom, Margie.

"Well, Margie's at the hospital right now. No big deal. Just routine tests. She'll be out today, I know she'd love to see you," John said.

"Okay, I'll take Amtrak down. I have some e-mail to catch up on and going along the coast will be fun." I got John to give me the number of the hospital where Margie was getting her tests so I could call and let her know I was coming.

When I called the hospital, they put me through to her doctor.

"I'm so sorry," the doctor said when he heard I was Margie's stepdaughter. "Margie has been diagnosed with terminal cancer and has decided to forgo any treatment. Because we can no longer help her, someone will need to come pick her up and take her home immediately."

"How long does she have?" I asked, in shock.

"About five to six months. Will you be the one who will be coming for her?" he replied.

You can never know what will show up in your life. You can only stay open to what is required of you in the present moment. When you let go of the way *you* think things should be and open yourself to the way they are appearing, you open yourself to the will of God, to the perfect organizing power of Nature.

That's what Janet did, and we'll tell you about the amazing miracles that occurred as a result, but first we need to help you create your Markers.

Markers are one more step in gaining increasing clarity.

Dr. Pankaj Naram is a famous Ayurvedic physician and pulse reader for the Dalai Lama. When Pankaj was in his twenties he was, in his own words, "a nobody, who knew nothing, and had nothing."

At that time, his teacher asked him what in his life was most important to him. Pankaj said, "To be the most renowned Ayurvedic physician in the world, making Ayurveda available to people throughout the world."

His teacher told him, "Okay, then write it down." Pankaj wrote it down, and his teacher then asked him, "How will you know when you are living this dream?"

Pankaj thought for a few minutes and said, "I will take the pulse of at least 100,000 people; Mother Teresa will come to my clinic and acknowledge my work; I will take the pulse of the Dalai Lama; and I will have Ayurvedic centers all over the world."

His teacher said, "Okay, write it down." Pankaj thought to himself, "How will I, a nobody, ever accomplish any of these things?" But he loved and respected his teacher so he wrote them down.

Now, more than two decades later, Pankaj has taken the pulse of over 400,000 people; Mother Teresa did come to his clinic in the eighties and praise him for his great work with AIDS; he is now called on to take the pulse of the Dalai Lama; and he has Ayurvedic centers in twelve countries around the world.

How did this happen?

Everything made by man is created first in someone's mind; then it becomes manifest in the world. Look around the room where you are sitting right now.

See that lamp? It began with Thomas Edison's lightbulb, which was based on Humphry Davy's idea that electricity could be used to heat a filament that would produce light. Then someone else had the thought, "Let me design this beautiful (or practical) lamp that will work with that lightbulb." Someone else had the thought, "How can we make thousands of these, distribute them to thousands of people, and make a good profit?" Then you had the thought, "I like this lamp. It will look nice in our house."

Because of all these thoughts, the lamp in your room got to you. It started just as an idea and eventually became a concrete reality in your life.

Every single thing you can see that was created by man was

an idea in someone's mind at one time. If you want to create the life of your dreams, it begins by writing your dreams down and becoming as clear as possible about them.

The power of intention and attention is what brings ideas into concrete form. When you have intention and attention with no tension, then the whole process becomes fun.

Intention

Intention—is the conscious or unconscious choice to create.

All of us are constantly creating the circumstances and situations in our world by virtue of the beliefs and concepts we hold to be true.

For most people, creations are unconscious, and so they view themselves as the victims of their situations and circumstances.

However, successful people know the secret—they create their reality from what they put their attention on. In this book, we use "intention" to mean the choices you make to create your world.

Some people state intentions and then are perplexed when the results in their life don't match their stated intentions. Why would that happen?

Here is a secret that could be worth a lifetime of fulfillment to you, so pay close attention:

**Your results will *always* match
your true intentions.**

Your life will always express what is going on deep inside you. Therefore, if your results are out of line with your stated intentions, it's time to do some self-examination.

Does this mean "bad" things don't happen to "good" people? Will good intentions keep you from being trapped in a hurricane or prevent your home from being destroyed by fire? Let's assume the answer is no.

Imagine two people are trapped in rising floodwaters from a huge storm. One is intent on ensuring his own survival and is giving his full attention to all the threats to his life. He doesn't care about anyone else. He may even save himself at the expense of others. The other is intent on giving love and helping those around her. Her full attention is on how she can give her love, her support, and her assistance to the people with whom she is trapped.

How do you think these two people will experience their lives in the midst of this catastrophe? The first is filled with fear, thinking about himself, and desperate to save himself. The second is so immersed in helping others that all she experiences is the love that is flowing between her and those she is assisting. She doesn't have time to worry and fret about the dangers because her attention is focused on giving and receiving love.

Will she be saved? Wouldn't you do everything in your power to save such a person? And whether she survives or not, what are the results? She provides and receives comfort. She is filled with love. She gives and receives help. She enjoys a quality of life that transcends the significance of physical survival.

In a more mundane example, some years ago we partnered with some friends to create a business. Together we stated our intention to generate $10 million in revenues and over $2 million in profits the first year. A year later we were $100,000 in debt after generating $1 million in revenues.

We stated our intentions clearly, we made a detailed plan, we executed the plan, and we worked our tails off. What went wrong?

Later, when we looked back over that time, we realized that our *real* intention was to make our partners happy by agreeing to what they wanted. There were many times when we felt something should be done differently, but because we believed they were more experienced in that arena, we decided it wasn't our place to change the way things were done.

In the short term, we did make them happy. We did things they liked, but in the end all of us were disappointed in the results.

Your results will *always* match your true intentions.

This means that if you want to know what is going on at the deepest level of your life, look to your results. When your results are out of line with your stated intentions, look more deeply to discover your real intentions, and then work on changing those to change the way you experience life.

When your actions are aligned with your intentions you will create your world out of those intentions.

Attention

Attention—is subjective awareness directed to an object. All of us give attention to something in every waking moment of the day. Life changes when the object of your attention becomes your conscious choice.

However, most people don't pay much attention to where they are placing their attention. Their lives are an unconscious stream of thoughts.

Most people's lives are directed by habit. Do you have a routine you follow when you get up in the morning? What about when you drive to work or to the store? Have you ever had the experience of driving somewhere familiar and discovering you've arrived without remembering how you got there? You've driven that route so many times that it has become a habit, and meanwhile your mind was engrossed in thought (i.e., your attention was on other things).

You can use the fact that we are habitual beings to your advantage. Begin to cultivate success habits.

What are success habits?

- Taking time daily to review your top five passions
- Choosing in favor of your passions whenever you're faced with a decision
- Taking responsibility for the life you've created
- Taking time daily for prayer and/or meditation
- Getting regular exercise
- Getting adequate rest
- Charitable giving on a regular basis
- Eating healthy foods that support clarity
- Speaking positively and uplifting others through your speech

What others can you think of?

Research has found that it takes twenty-one days to create a new habit. Don't try to do everything at once. Choose one new habit, master it, then move on to another.

What was that mantra we taught you earlier?

What you put your attention on
grows stronger in your life.

The second step in manifesting anything is to put attention on its creation. This means developing the habit of giving attention to everything that supports your intention and being indifferent to those things that do not.

A great teacher once said, "Indifference is the weapon to be used for any negative situation in life."

Put your attention on all the good in your life, deal with situations that must be dealt with, and don't dwell on anything that doesn't support what you choose to create.

When Janet found out she needed to put her own plans on hold to look after her stepmother, she could have convinced herself that her dream would never be realized. Had she done that, we probably wouldn't be telling you her amazing story now.

Instead, she focused on what needed to be done in that moment, and it turned out this apparent block in the road was to become a huge gift—in a number of ways.

Unfortunately, most people focus their attention on all the reasons their dreams won't come true. Why? Because they're afraid they won't get what they want. If you think some people are just too lazy to pursue their dreams, you'll find that this laziness is a mask for the fear of failure they hold deep inside.

When you are consumed by fear, when your attention is on the things that are going wrong in your life, you create inactivity and boredom or, even worse, you create the things you fear will happen to you.

Yet all of us feel fear from time to time. What do you do when the fear hits?

Facing Fear—The Head-on Approach

If you're like Tellman Knudson of ListCrusade.com, you get excited and push through the fear to the goal. When Tellman was about twenty-seven, he decided he wanted to create a multimillion-dollar Internet marketing business that showed people how to build a massive e-mail list (one of the critical factors for success on the Internet). At the time, his office consisted of a makeshift cubicle in his living room, with only a rattling, rusty fan to cool him off in the hot summer and a CD-ROM drive that he had to take out of his computer and shake in order to play a CD.

A part of Tellman was scared to death; another part of him was completely exhilarated by the challenge. He put his attention on the exhilaration. He wrote e-mails to over sixty of the top Internet marketers on the Web. Months went by. Most of them never responded. He kept at it. Eventually, he created relationships with some of them, including Ric Thompson, our partner at *Healthy Wealthy nWise*.

In his first three months after launching ListCrusade.com, Tellman had built an e-mail list of over 25,000 and had made over $200,000 in sales. After nine months he had topped $800,000 in sales. Within two years he had generated over $2 million in sales.

This only happened because Tellman directed his attention toward what got him excited, not toward what scared him.

Facing Fear—The Step-by-Step Approach

If you're not like Tellman, and you find that fear immobilizes you, then take small steps toward your goal. Each small step achieved will build your confidence and reduce the fear until you get to the point where you're able to push through the last bit of fear and get on to the result.

With each step, put your attention on what you've already accomplished. Some people find affirmations helpful, like: "I am capable and successful in achieving my goals."

We find it more useful to turn the affirmation into a question: "What is there about me that could make me successful in achieving my goals?" The mind is an amazing machine. Ask it a question and it will search for an answer. If you ask a question like this and can't come up with an answer, then find a friend who values and appreciates you. Ask them to tell you the answer. We guarantee they will.

Don't be surprised if they tell you things you didn't even know about yourself, like you're comfortable to be around, or they feel happier when they spend time with you, or they know they can count on you, or you help them look at things differently.

If you don't see the good in you, it's only because you've gotten into the habit of criticizing yourself. Now is the time to change that habit. Remember what we said about it taking twenty-one days to change a habit?

Post these questions where you can see them each day, and every day for at least twenty-one days, take a few minutes to write down things you appreciate about yourself. This is so important we have formalized it in our own lives and call it the Appreciation Game. We'll share all the details in chapter 7.

You will find that by putting your attention on your strengths, how capable you are, and the reasons you can accomplish your goals, fear will drop away. With remarkable ease, the results you desire will begin showing up in your life.

No Tension

No tension—means exactly that. Creating intentions and putting your attention on them is a simple, easy, effortless
process.

No matter where you are or what you're going through,
you are creating your world through what you put your attention on. You don't have to try. You do it naturally.

It doesn't matter whether you're in the midst of a disaster, a
single mother on welfare, or a billionaire real estate tycoon.
Every day you create your experience of life from what you
give your attention to.

It's a choice. Yet most people don't choose. They uncon-
sciously allow their attention to go to the things they fear the
most. And guess what shows up in their lives? That's right.
The things they fear the most.

The person caught in the midst of a disaster can choose to
focus on the fear of being killed or on how he can help those
around him who need assistance. The single mother on welfare can choose to focus on the fear that she won't have enough
food for her babies, or she can focus on the things she can do
for her babies. The billionaire real estate tycoon can focus on
the fear that his fortune will be wiped out, or he can focus
on the good he can do with his wealth.

When you become conscious of where you're putting your
attention, it is no more difficult than being unconscious about
it. The difference is that now you are aware of what you are
creating.

If you want to see how powerful you are, look at your life

and what you've created, good or otherwise. It is your creation. Here's the good news: if you're not happy with what you've created, you can begin creating consciously now.

Your passion list and all the other tools we'll share with you in the coming chapters are there to inspire you, excite you, and remind you of what's truly important to you in your life. They are there to help you put your attention on the things that will bring more joy and fulfillment into your life.

If you ever find yourself not wanting to read your passions or review your goals or go over your vision, it means either you've been straining on these things or there is an underlying fear that you can't have or achieve what you have written.

When you are truly passionate about something, there is nothing that can keep you from it. You won't have to try to put your attention on it, because it draws you irresistibly to it.

"I tried everything I could think of to get Janet focused on other projects, but nothing could take her attention off her trip to India," Chris will tell you. There wasn't any question about it. From Janet's side, there was no effort involved whatsoever. It was as if this passion drew her inextricably onward of its own volition.

When you write out your passions in a way that excites you, when your goals are lofty yet achievable, when your vision is aligned with your heart's deepest purpose, then these things will draw you naturally to them. You will look forward to reading through them. When you feel down, you'll be drawn to reviewing them because they will pick you up again.

When your thoughts are aligned with the deepest stirrings in your heart, intention, attention, and no tension are completely natural and effortless.

Your Markers

Dr. Naram knew he was passionate about becoming the most renowned Ayurvedic physician and making Ayurveda known throughout the world. With the help of his teacher, he then identified the "Markers" or "Signposts" that would allow him to know he is really living that passion.

From his perspective, taking the pulse of the Dalai Lama, being acknowledged by Mother Teresa, treating over 100,000 people, and having Ayurvedic clinics all over the world were completely outside the realm of the possible when he first wrote them down. Yet he just innocently took his teacher's advice and wrote out the things he'd love to create in his life (his intentions). Then he kept these Markers in mind (in his attention) while he built his Ayurvedic practice. He didn't strain after them. He simply allowed them to show up in their own perfect timing (no tension). And show up they did!

Now we are giving you that same opportunity. Take a blank piece of paper and write one of your passions at the top of the paper. Then write out three to five Markers describing what will have happened when you are fully living your passion. These are the things that will tell you that your passion is alive and well in your life.

Please don't think about how your Markers will be achieved. Just write them out. Here is an example:

Passion: *I am a world-renowned concert pianist.*

Markers:

1. I have performed for heads of state all over the world
2. I have performed with the New York Philharmonic orchestra
3. I have my own television special
4. I earn over $1 million a year from my performances

Passion: *I am living in the moment and trusting my intuition.*

Markers:

1. I am fully present with each person I meet and with whom I spend time
2. I experience every day as perfect, and the days seem to flow effortlessly
3. I have a clear internal sense about what action is the best for me at every moment
4. Others remark on my confidence and how wonderful it is to be around me

All right, now it's your turn. Create a page for each of your passions and write out your Markers for each of them. Keep these pages because in the next chapter you'll be using them again.

And remember, things frequently don't turn out the way you think they will. Taking care of her stepmother was definitely *not* one of Janet's Markers for spending time with the enlightened. Staying open, she chose in favor of her passions and little did she guess . . .

ALLOWING THE DREAM
TO COME ALIVE

Every moment is a gift, when we stay open
to what is appearing now.
—*Janet and Chris Attwood*

After hearing that my stepmother needed someone to
look after her, I knew this was what I had to do. Staying
open to what was appearing moment by moment, I put
aside my dreams of being with the enlightened and
moved in with Margie, who had now become my #1
passion.

That was one of the most beautiful times I've ever
had. The minute I walked into Margie's house I felt a
sense of elation. I was so clear that this opportunity to
be with her in her last days was a gift. We had been
through so much together.

I told her how happy I was that I got to be the one to

take care of her, and her response brought tears to my eyes.

"Oh Janet, thank you. That makes me so happy. I was so afraid I would be a burden."

The house was overflowing with love.

I was shocked when, after less than a week, Margie's condition deteriorated dramatically. She seemed to be leaving much more quickly than the five or six months the doctor said she had left.

On the fifth day after I arrived, Margie passed away quietly and peacefully. While my sister was overseas, my brother, John, and I dealt with taking care of Margie's body and her estate.

Before Margie passed away, I asked if I could create a special ceremony for her after her passing. I told her I had learned from my spiritual teachers that it takes a number of days for the soul to leave the body. To make sure the transition is smooth, friends and family should pray, meditate, sing spiritual songs, and read spiritual literature in the presence of the deceased. Margie loved the idea and said she would be honored if I did those things for her after she died.

My niece, Tonia, and I bathed Margie and dressed her in her favorite clothes. We collected hundreds of flowers from the neighborhood and then placed them all over her from head to toe, with just her beautiful face beaming out amongst them. My brother and I gathered all of Margie's plants as well as favorite pictures of those she loved and placed them all around her. Then we lit candles and incense and created the most celestial environment for her.

During the next day we meditated and prayed, read spiritual literature, and played Margie her favorite music. John even insisted on watching the golf tournament and turned the volume up so Margie could hear just in case she was listening. "Golf," John said, "was Margie's favorite sport."

It happened on the second day after her passing that one of my friends who had lived in India for many years e-mailed me that a great Saint called Bapuji was in Orange County, about three hours away, and I had to go meet him for my documentary. She didn't know my stepmother had just passed away.

When I let her know what was going on, she gave me the phone number to contact one of Bapuji's devotees. My thought was, "Maybe he can tell me if there is anything more I should do for Margie."

I called and got to talk with Bapuji, whose full name is Prem Avadhoot Maharaj, through a translator. After talking with this great Saint for a few minutes, his devotee told me, "Bapuji wants you to know there is a 99 percent chance he will come tomorrow to bless your stepmother."

I was completely blown away. The next day, at the appointed time, a car drove up, and a beautiful, elderly Indian Saint draped in the traditional white Indian clothing called a dhoti got out of the car with his arms full of roses. Those who accompanied him carried a huge basket of fruit.

Bapuji surveyed the room that Margie was in and smiled. I could tell he was pleased with all we had done for her so far. He carefully handed both my brother and me a rose and had us gently place them across Margie's body. When we were done, Bapuji stood in silence next to Margie for a long time. Then he motioned to my brother and me to sit down on the floor, and he proceeded to sit next to us on the couch. He spent the next two hours in silence, gently stroking our heads and showering both of us with love.

When Bapuji was done, he walked to his car, turned to my brother and me, and said, "Do you know why I have come?"

"No" I said.

"It was not because of you."

"I didn't think so," I replied.

Then Bapuji looked at us with the most compassionate, loving eyes and in a gentle voice said, "I came because when you were telling me about your stepmother I felt such a deep connection that I felt she might have been my mother in a past life."

My passion to spend time with the enlightened was beginning to be realized, in a way I could never have possibly imagined.

This or Something Better!

I t was a shock to Janet when Margie passed. It happened so quickly and unexpectedly.

It was an equally big shock when her brother told her a week later that Margie had left a significant estate and Janet would be receiving a large amount of money very soon.

Suddenly, all the money she needed for her trip to India was available—a gift from her beloved Margie. And so you see why we say, "This or something better!" at the bottom of our Passion Cards.

Janet's experience illustrates one of the most important secrets we have to share with you. When you are clear about *what* your passions are, you can't predict *how* they will get fulfilled.

Okay, we can hear you saying, "That was just a fortunate coincidence. I don't have any rich relatives who are about to die and leave *me* a bunch of money!"

This is the point exactly. You can't imagine in advance *how* your passions will get fulfilled. It never occurred to Janet that Margie might pass away and leave her money. Margie's death was completely unexpected.

Janet couldn't have figured out how she would receive more than enough money to fulfill her passion. What was required of her was to remain open to everything that appeared, without holding on to her own concepts of what she needed.

There are many ways in which the means of fulfilling your passions can show up. Most of us have been taught that when you want to achieve something, you have to make a plan, execute your plan, and then, if you do a good job, you'll enjoy the results.

That may well be exactly how it works for you, and it could also be that in spite of your best-laid plans, nothing seems to go the way you expected. In these moments, beware the tendency to think there is only one way your dreams can be fulfilled.

What is required of you is to stay open. Realize that the good in your life may not appear in the ways you think it will. When things happen that are not what you had planned, expected, or wanted, let go of your own will and open up to God's will, to that perfect organizing power of Nature. Watch how your life unfolds, and accept what appears now.

When her stepmother needed her, Janet realized her passion to give love and support to her family was more important in that moment than spending time with the enlightened. Yet as it turned out, the love she showered on Margie was the ground on which an enlightened Saint appeared in her life.

Before we tell you about Janet's unbelievable adventures in India, which grew out of the simple process of writing down what she loves the most, let's create your Vision Board and your Passion Pages, and write your 100th birthday speech.

Your Vision Board

Our friend John Assaraf lives near San Diego, California, in a gorgeous home on six mountaintop acres surrounded by 320 fruitbearing orange trees, with incredible panoramic views. He is a millionaire many times over from his business successes.

Years ago when John was living in Indiana, he created a Vision Board—a board of all the things he wanted to create in his life, from pictures he had cut out of magazines. One of the pictures on that board was of his dream home.

He put his Vision Board up in his office and kept it there for about two years as an ongoing reminder of the things he was choosing to create. After that year he put the Vision Boards away and never looked at them again.

About five years later, John and his family had moved to the beautiful home he now owns near San Diego. When the movers brought the sealed boxes that held his Vision Boards to the new house, he put them aside in his office to open later. One early morning, his son came into his office and noticed the sealed boxes and said, "Daddy, what's this?"

"These are Vision Boards I made before you were born of all the things I wanted to have someday."

As John pulled out one of the boards to show his son, he was shocked. John looked at the board he was holding and saw the picture he had pasted on it so many years ago was a picture of the very house he and his family were now living in! He had completely forgotten about the board and the specific house he had put on it by the time he went to buy his dream home. Yet, somehow, his mind drew him to the house he had selected as his perfect home.

We tell you this story for two reasons. First and foremost, never underestimate the power of the mind to create the vision you hold. Second, creating a Vision Board is one of the most fun things you can do to begin creating the life of your dreams.

You can get some poster board or do as Chris does and paste your pictures on a large mirror. The advantage of the latter approach is that it's easy to add and change pictures over time. Janet pastes her pictures in a notebook so she can sit and look at them from time to time and take them with her.

Whichever approach you take, get a big pile of magazines on topics related to your passions and start going through them. Or you can search the Internet to find the pictures you want.

Cut out pictures of the things you want to be, do, or have, and paste them on your Vision Board. Put the board somewhere where you'll see it daily. You have created a simple set of pictures to remind you of what you choose to create in your life. Remember that mantra we taught you?

**What you put your attention on grows stronger in
your life.**

A Vision Board is one of the easy ways to keep your attention on the things you really want to grow stronger in your life.

Your Passion Pages

Was that fun? Of course if you're like us you're still reading the book and haven't yet done the Vision Board.

Just remember, the people who are most successful at living passionate lives are the ones who take the time to do their inner homework.

Creating a Vision Board is the kind of thing that's really fun to do with friends. So if you haven't made your Vision Board yet, throw a vision party and create your board with a bunch of your best buddies.

Let's see, what have we accomplished so far? You have:

- Your top five passions
- Your Passion Cards posted in strategic locations
- Your Markers
- Your Vision Board

Why have you been doing these things?

> **When you are clear,**
> **what you want will show up in your life,**
> **and only to the extent you are clear.**

Are you beginning to get a clearer idea of what your life might look like when you're living your passions? Let's take it to another level and create your Passion Pages.

In chapter 5 you created a page for each of your top five passions and wrote down Markers for each one. Now on that same page write a few paragraphs describing what that passion means to you.

Close your eyes for a minute. Imagine what life is like for you when you are completely living this passion. What does it feel like? How do your days change when you're living this passion fully? Are there any changes in the ways you interact with others? What impact does this passion have on your life?

Once you have a clear picture of life when you're living this passion, begin writing.

Do this now.

When you've written a page on each of your top five passions, take a break. When you come back to these sheets in a few minutes or an hour or tomorrow, read them out loud to yourself.

Begin by reading your five passions. How does that feel? Now read each page you've written on each passion. At the end of each page, stop, close your eyes, and picture your life as you've just written it. How does that feel?

Another principle:

**Your life is created first in your mind,
then in the world.**

Will your life look exactly as you picture it now? Of course not! It will be better.

The purpose of writing out these pages is to uplift your vision, inspire you, and move your heart to go places you would not have otherwise been able to go.

Your life will always be better than you can imagine it now, because you are beginning to consciously create that life. Your future life will be the result of all the evolution and growth you have experienced between now and then.

Your life becomes seemingly worse when you are intent on it appearing the way *you* think it should be. When you insist that the world conform to your concepts of what is best, and it doesn't, what happens? You suffer.

Everything in your life is structured for your evolution. The laws of nature that govern every aspect of existence, including our daily lives, are designed to support you in experiencing deeper aspects of your own nature.

When you fight reality, you will lose—always. When you realize that every part of your life is working to bring you closer to knowing your true nature more completely, life can only get better.

By staying open to how life is appearing at this moment, free of your concepts of how it "should" be, you create the opportunity for miracles to occur.

Your 100th Birthday

Now we're going to pull all the pieces together into one grand vision of your life. Today you have the chance to travel in time to your 100th birthday, to a time years from now when you are looking back on your whole life.

Imagine it's that day. Your friends and family have come together from all over to be with you. On this day your spouse or your best friend is going to give a speech honoring you for all you have given and shared with those around you over the long course of your life.

And you're going to write that speech now.

What is the legacy you want to create in your life? How do you want people to remember you? Your 100th birthday speech will draw on everything you've done up until now, your passions list, your Markers, your Vision Board, and your Passion Pages, to summarize a life well lived. When you have completed your 100th birthday speech it should include everything you have written up until now, because you *can* have everything you choose to have in your life.

When you write this speech, write it in the third person, just as if your best friend or spouse had written it about you, your life, and the influence you've had.

This is your chance to let loose and talk about the kind of life you truly choose to create. Imagine yourself at that birthday party. What will your life look like from that vantage point, when you have lived the kind of life you will feel great about? Who have you loved and who has loved you? What did you create and what did you teach through your living? Why will people be thankful to have known you?

Your 100th birthday speech will probably be quite a few pages. After all it describes the contributions of your entire life. Here is a short sample of a few of the things Chris might say about Janet on her 100th birthday, to help get you started:

Thank you all for coming to the heartland of America, Fairfield, Iowa, to this place that Janet has helped make a model of ideal living, to celebrate a life that has affected people everywhere. It's not surprising that there are over five thousand people here to celebrate the 100th birthday of this beautiful woman who has touched so many hearts.

Many of you have traveled far distances to be here: from the heights of the Himalayas to the mountaintops of Nepal to the great cities of Europe, South America, Australia, New Zealand, Asia, and Africa. Janet's life has been an inspiration for all of us who are committed to living a passionate, fully enlightened life.

Janet has proven through her own example that miracles happen over and over and over again when we commit ourselves fully to living our passions. Her books, her weekly TV show, her films, her magazines and radio programs have all had one theme: Your passions are the clues to your personal destiny.

And how appropriate that Janet's life should be dedicated to teaching all of us how to live with passion, when that is what her own life expresses so completely. Passion springs from the heart, and it is the quality of her beautiful, all-encompassing heart that has touched millions and made her TV show the #1 rated show worldwide.

That same beautiful, loving heart connected with filmgoers and won her an Academy Award for her groundbreaking documentary that brought living Saints from around the world into the homes of people in every country.

Those who know her, affectionately call her Jani Ma because she has truly been a great mother to all of us, showing us how to discern our personal destinies and live a life of real service.

Even as she has enjoyed great commercial success, Janet has been an inspiration for her philanthropy. Serving as a role model of a "reverse tither," she donates 90 percent of her income each year to causes that raise the quality of life in the world.

Long after she has left her physical body, Janet's influence will be felt through the work of her foundations and the billions of dollars they distribute each year to improve lives through preventive health care programs, organic agriculture programs, education programs, financial self-sufficiency programs, community planning programs, scientific research programs, programs for the arts, and programs for uplifting human consciousness.

This is a brief sample of a 100th birthday speech. Remember you are unique. Your passions are leading you to express *your* unique gifts. You are you, so your speech will not sound like Janet's or Chris's or anyone else's. It is uniquely yours.

Not everyone's passions will lead to a speech that embodies such lofty ideals as Janet's, and some could sound more like this (as you read, think about what you'll say in your speech):

What a delight it is to be here with all those who have been touched by John. John's life has been a life of love.

He loves his family. He loves the ocean. He loves nature. He loves to just meet people at the docks and hang out with them. He can meet anyone and really see who they are. Before they know it they'll be sharing their life's story. John has that unique ability to make everyone feel like they are special and that their life is worth living.

His huge heart flows in all directions. During some of this past century's great disasters, John went into the midst of the devastation handing out twenty-dollar bills. He saw that with all the assistance the survivors received, none of it provided the relief of having a few dollars in their pockets.

John is loyal beyond words. Time and time again he has extended himself to help his beautiful wife, Anne, his kids, his sisters, and the friends who fill up his life.

John has always followed his heart. He found a way to merge his love of the ocean with his need for a place to live and a source of income. For years he has lived on his boats. His skill in finding old, battered boats with lots of potential has allowed him to create great deals for his customers while making a great living himself from fixing up the boats he loves so much.

It's so appropriate that John should be surrounded by the family, friends, and loved ones to whom he has given so much.

Your 100th birthday speech is your chance to express the reason you were put on this earth, to describe how you have given, are giving, and will continue to give your gifts to the world. Write it down and see how it makes you feel.

Do it now!

All of the exercises in this book have one purpose in mind: to create clarity about what you would like your life to be.

While you appear to be writing about the future as you write your 100th birthday speech, you are not. You are writing down your thoughts, dreams, and vision as they exist in this snapshot of time.

When your 100th birthday comes, we guarantee your life will look different from what you have written today. What you write is not about the future because there is no way you can know what the future will be. Your writing today is about your thoughts and feelings *now*.

This process will draw to you more joy, more abundance, more success, more peace, more delight, more of whatever it is you desire. And the specifics of what that looks like, when the future becomes today, are part of the mystery of life.

That's why, at the end of each of the things we write or draw, we always put:

This or something better!

As she took The Passion Test in 2003, Janet couldn't have imagined what "better" meant when she expressed the desire to spend time with the enlightened. Boy, was she in for a surprise!

THE WORLD IS
AS YOU ARE

He who has a why to live for can bear almost any how.
—*Friedrich Nietzsche*

With the finances taken care of for my trip to India, it was just a matter of organizing the details. I reconnected with Juliann, who ordered all the video equipment we would need.

Then I contacted friends who I knew could point me toward the most enlightened teachers in India and Nepal. Using my natural talent for connecting, I got permission to interview a number of these teachers.

When I arrived in India, one of my first stops was a small village in the western part of the country, the home of Prem Avadhoot Maharaj, or Bapuji, the Saint who had visited to pay respects to my stepmom.

Bapuji invited us to be his personal guests in his home in a remote village, outside of Ahmedabad, called Linch. Aside from him, there were sixteen family members total. Sons, wives, children, and family friends all lived happily in Bapuji's home.

It was a beautiful home. Simple but very clean and orderly. Bapuji gave Juliann and me two rooms on the top floor, one to sleep in and the other to meditate in.

My first lesson was not far away.

Our first morning at Bapuji's house, I woke up at 4:30 a.m., while Juliann was sleeping, and decided to meditate. I took a candle into the meditation room, put it on what appeared to be a tabletop, and began my meditation.

After some time, I heard Juliann waking, so I went in to say good morning. As we were sitting on the bed laughing at how normal we felt in this strange environment with these Indians who couldn't speak very much English, we both started to smell smoke. I looked around, and through the door to the meditation room I saw flames enveloping the room.

"Oh my God," I said, "the room is on fire!" My head swirling, I went into action mode. I immediately remembered that the upstairs bathroom had two buckets of water, since there was no running water anywhere upstairs.

Terrified of burning down Bapuji's house and everyone in it, I screamed at Juliann, "We have to get the water buckets—*now*!" We ran to the bathroom, grabbed the two buckets of water and poured them all over the burning objects in the meditation room as the fire was quickly starting to envelop one wall.

My one and only thought was, "No way am I going to burn down Bapuji's house!"

I ran into our bedroom and grabbed my pillow. With Juliann yelling at me to get out of the burning room or I would die, I furiously fought back the flames, hitting them ferociously with the pillow, hoping for a miracle to occur.

As I was being overtaken by smoke, Juliann, fearing for my life and the lives of everyone in the house, ran out of the room screaming at the top of her lungs, "Fire, fire!" Not knowing what the word *fire* meant, Bapuji's sons took a while to understand.

As soon as everyone in the house realized what she was screaming about, buckets started arriving from everywhere. In no time, the fire was put out.

Even before the fire was out, Juliann and I were surrounded by the wives and children and Bapuji, making sure that we were okay. In all the chaos I was acutely aware that there was absolutely no concern from anyone for the house, the burned room, or whatever belongings had been destroyed.

After making sure Juliann and I had not been hurt, the family members took a quick survey of the damage. One wall and eight very large overstuffed suitcases of the family's belongings were destroyed. I was devastated.

Once Bapuji and the others made sure a second, third, and fourth time that Juliann and I were okay, a huge roar of laughter filled the house.

We just stood there dumbstruck. Juliann and I had no idea what they were laughing about.

Bapuji walked up to us and said, "Please don't feel

bad, this was a blessing," and walked away smiling. All the other family members smiled in agreement as Juliann and I listened with our mouths open.

Tears streaming down my face, I looked at Juliann and said, "Who are these people?"

In my humble state, all I could feel was blessed. Blessed to witness what real love in action looks like. I had almost burned down the home in which Bapuji's family had always lived, and the only comments from them were, "Are you okay?" and quickly following, "It was a blessing!"

How can it possibly be a blessing for your belongings to go up in smoke? Bapuji and his family understand that for the new to be created, the old must be destroyed. Because life is constantly evolving, hanging on to the old may prevent the new from coming in.

Bapuji and his family also view all acts of creation and destruction as acts of God, for they believe God is good and God is everything. There can be no thought of being a victim, for they know that all of God's acts are blessings.

This is the same idea that is conveyed in the Bible: "Give thanks in all circumstances, for this is God's will for you" (I Thess. 5:18).

On this note Janet's adventures in India and Nepal began. In a little while we'll share why Janet came home saying this was "the best experience of my life," but first we want to give you some tools you'll find helpful on the path to your passionate life.

In coaching thousands of people on The Passion Test, the one thing we can be sure we'll find when someone is having a hard time believing they could fulfill their passions is a good ol' case of "low self-esteem."

Have you ever noticed that when someone is feeling badly about themselves, no matter how much you tell them how beautiful they are, how great they are, and how much you love them they just can't hear it? What accompanies low self-esteem is the belief that "I am not worthy and therefore I can't possibly fulfill my dreams."

Earlier we promised to share the secrets we've learned for taking care of the "how" part of fulfilling your passions, once you're clear on the "what." You may remember that Janet began thinking of a number of ways to get herself to India. Yet looking back, we can see that the "how" appeared in ways she could never have figured out on her own. The "how" of living your passions is the result of being aligned with the flow of natural law, with your "higher self."

In this chapter we will share a powerful tool and some fundamental principles we've found essential for connecting with your higher self—that part of you which is capable of achieving all of your dreams and allowing you to give all of your gifts fully.

The Appreciation Game (from Janet)

For years I suffered from low self-esteem. I could go into all of the reasons why, but in the spirit of being proactive I'd rather share with you a tool my friend Marie Diamond suggested to me many years ago that truly helped transform the way I saw myself.

Chris and I call it the Appreciation Game.

Every day I would review what I had done that day and somehow find something I appreciated about myself. It didn't matter if it seemed like a small thing. The exercise was to find something I could appreciate about myself, no matter what.

At first this exercise wasn't so easy. I soon started to see how there was a payoff for me every time I allowed myself to feel like a victim. It was interesting what showed up as I looked at why I wasn't appreciating myself and instead chose to feel like I wasn't worthy or capable or lovable, etc.

I discovered the payoff (and there is always a payoff) of being victimized was that I:

1. got people's attention
2. got their sympathy
3. got to give up
4. got to feel not worthy
5. and the list went on

Pretty scary stuff, wouldn't you agree? Finally, after many starts and stops playing the Appreciation Game, I finally kicked my low self-esteem addiction and chose instead to put my attention not only on my passions but also on my achievements.

In my seminars, to illustrate the importance of this point, I share the story Mark Victor Hansen and Bob Allen told me about a study done on two bowling teams.

Bowling team A bowled a game and received a video edited to show only the things they did wrong. The bowlers were told to study the video to improve their game.

Bowling team B bowled a game and received a video edited

to show only the bowlers' best performances. Both teams were told to study the video to improve their game.

The two teams bowled again. What were the results? Both teams improved, but improvements in the team that focused on their best performances were far greater.

Got the point? Give your attention to what you do right, to your wins, to the things you do well. You will find your improvement is faster and much greater than when you try to fix your mistakes.

Now about this word *mistake*.

How about looking at that word once again?

Mis-take.

Are you having an *aha* moment yet?

Mis-take, as in take one, take two, take three, and so on.

That's right, it's just one "take." You get another chance to do it again! How far out is that? I bet you always thought you were doing it wrong when all along there was just another way that might serve you and all concerned better. Now that is good!

Okay, back to the Appreciation Game. You can play this game on your own or with a partner (it's really fun to play it with a partner who truly loves and appreciates you).

On your own, sit for a few minutes at the end of the day or first thing in the morning. Make a list of at least ten things you appreciate about yourself, what you accomplished that day, or wins that showed up in your life that day. Don't repeat any of the things that were on your list on previous days.

Do this every day for a week and see how you're feeling about yourself. You'll get the greatest benefit when you write out your lists.

Not only does writing down your Appreciation Game allow you to actually see all the great things you have done and been, but the greatness of you will go in more deeply and your mind will begin to reverse the self-deprecating talk that prevents you from realizing your dreams.

If you are playing the Appreciation Game with a partner, prepare to have some fun. Take turns. You find one thing you appreciate about the other and let them know. Then the other person takes their turn to find something they love about you. Do this ten times.

Now do another round, except this time each person says one thing they appreciate about themself, and they can't repeat anything that has already been said. Notice how you feel after playing the Appreciation Game—about yourself and about your partner.

The Seven Keys to Living Life Aligned with Passion

The ability to live life in accord with higher principles is one of the things that distinguishes humans from other animals.

We have discovered there are certain key principles that are essential to living a passionate life. We share them with you here.

1. Commitment. Until you are committed, nothing will happen for you. There is nothing more important to creating your passionate life than your unshakable commitment to choosing in favor of your passions. Every day you will be asked to put other things ahead of the things you love most. Keep your passions where you can see them, and learn to say no lovingly. Here's one line you can practice:

> **"I so appreciate your asking,**
> **and I'm not able to do that now."**

Be sure to use *and* rather than *but*. *And* connects you with the other person, while *but* separates.

Vary the words to make them appropriate. Just remember to first appreciate, love, understand, and value the other person; then state what you need.

Lastly, keep in mind point 4 below (Stay Open). What's most important may shift temporarily in the light of urgent circumstances. When Janet found out Margie might not have long to live, her love for her stepmother took precedence over spending time with the enlightened. So be committed, and be prepared to be flexible.

2. Clarity. When you are clear, what you want will show up in your life, and only to the extent that you are clear. Have you heard that somewhere before? Fuzzy desires give fuzzy results. Use the tools in this book plus any others you find and enjoy to get absolutely clear about what you choose to create in your life. Then realize gaining clarity is not a one-time experience, it's an ongoing process. Take The Passion Test at least every six months and review your Markers and Passion Pages at least once a year.

3. Attention. What you put your attention on grows stronger in your life. We told you we were going to keep repeating these until they're embedded in your DNA! Pay attention every day, every moment, to what you are putting your attention on. You will attract all the people, places, and things you need to create those things to which you give attention. As you shift your focus to all the good that is flowing into your life, watch how your life is transformed.

4. Stay Open. Your greatest good may not be what you think it is. When you are open to whatever is appearing in this moment, even if it's different from what you think it should be, you release your individual will and open up to God's will for you. This is the path to living your highest purpose in life. This is also the secret to overcoming any obstacle that may arise in your life. When disaster strikes and you are open, you are able to take advantage of the opportunities that inevitably present themselves. By staying open, Janet was not only able to enjoy some of the sweetest moments of her life with Margie, she also was able to meet and welcome Bapuji into her home.

5. Integrity. Be as true to yourself as you are to others and as true to others as you are to yourself. The biggest challenge most of us face is to meet our responsibilities to others while pursuing our passions at the same time.

When you make commitments to others, make sure those commitments are aligned with your passions. Once you make commitments, keep them. If something else comes up, talk to the other person and ask their permission to renegotiate your commitment. If they aren't willing or able to make the necessary change, then keep your commitment as you originally made it—even if it is un-comfortable.

Do this a few times and you will become more careful about the commitments you make. And treat yourself with the same respect. When you make a commitment to yourself, treat it in the same way you would treat your commitment to another. That includes being willing to renegotiate your commitment when new circumstances arise.

Janet would not have been true to herself if she had ignored Margie's need and just said, "Sorry, I'm commit-ted to spending time with the enlightened so I can't help." In that moment, being with and caring for Margie meant much more to her than spending time with the enlight-ened. Be true to yourself, and when in doubt, practice principle 7 (Follow Your Heart).

6. Persistence. Many begin the journey. Those who finish it are the ones who achieve success and fulfillment in life. In his classic book *Think and Grow Rich*, Napoleon Hill tells the story of a man who bought property with the intention of mining gold. He discovered what appeared to be a massive vein. He went out and purchased the machinery to mine the gold, but before he made any significant prof-its, the vein dried up. He dug and dug, and then finally he gave up and sold the property and machinery for a few hundred dollars to a junk dealer.

That dealer consulted an expert who showed him that the previous owner had failed because he didn't under-stand the nature of fault lines. The expert told the new owner he would find the vein again, not far beyond where the digging had previously stopped. The new owner followed this expert advice, and sure enough found millions of dollars in gold just three feet beyond where the previous owner had stopped digging.

When you're living life truly aligned with your passions, persistence is not hard. You will find you can't stop, even if you want to. Your deepest passions will drive you in spite of yourself.

7. Follow Your Heart. When all else fails, listen to your heart. Passion emerges from the heart, not from the mind. When you feel confused or lost or don't know which direction to head, then just start walking and pay attention to what your heart tells you. Do what you love, follow your heart's direction, and the path to fulfillment in life will naturally unfold before you.

It Was the Best Experience of My Life

"How was your trip?" Chris asked.

"It was absolutely the best and most amazing experience of my entire life," Janet replied.

"What happened?"

A perplexed expression came over her face.

"I must be flippin' crazy!" she said.

In spite of all her trials, Janet's trip to India was the best experience of her life.

What made it the best? There was a passion that burned inside her every moment of the day. It didn't matter what was happening on the surface level of life. Sickness, falling off mountains, traveling alone, nothing could shake the love she felt for what she was doing.

This is one of those secrets you will want to take special note of:

When you are aligned with your deepest, most important passions, the ups and downs of daily life won't be able to throw you off track.

Here's what it was like in Janet's own words.

There is no way to adequately convey the profound experiences and life-transforming events that took place on this trip. But I want you to have a sense of the miracles that are possible when you give yourself over fully to your passions, so let me give you a taste of this remarkable adventure.

After the fire at Bapuji's house, Juliann and I headed for Nepal, where my mind would again be blown.

Every step of the journey was magical. First, a friend told us about a 107-year-old woman Saint. We went to visit her as she was saying her daily prayers. She paid no attention to us, even after we entered her room, until she had finished her daily ritual.

Then she turned and sang to us of beauty, love, and devotion to God. Sitting in this simple hut with this old woman, I felt more comfortable, more at ease, more honored, and more privileged than if I had been in the wealthiest palace with the greatest king on earth.

From there I trekked to the tops of mountains to visit Saints with my guide and camera equipment. I found myself in a hospital room with an Aghori master (the Aghori have a tradition that seeks liberation by embracing all things, including things most people in the world consider "bad" or "impure"). Everywhere I went, I was met with love.

You Are Not Your Body

Here's a tiny sampling of what these experiences were like. I had met the Aghori master a year before. He was the master of Dr. Pankaj Naram. Pankaj had told me story after story of the amazing mastery of this man. How, for example, he had Pankaj pick out three monkeys from hundreds that were running around. Then he repeated a specific mantra and those same three monkeys came and sat in front of him on the ground.

Pankaj explained that the Aghori was the master of specific sounds that create precise effects in the world, yet the Aghori turned away any who came to learn such things from him. The Aghori said that pursuit of powers was a waste of life. "Let man seek realization of the Self, and then whatever powers he may want will be his," was the Aghori's advice.

Pankaj had taken me to visit his Aghori master and explained sadly that the Aghori had acquired ear cancer at the moment he cured a devotee of this terrible disease. I asked Pankaj why this had happened, and he said he'd asked the same question of Aghori.

"It is my karma and my time to pass from this world," was his simple reply.

Now as I returned to Nepal, I visited this Aghori in the hospital and was completely melted by the love that met me. I had visited his home, and Pankaj had shown me how the Aghori felt such compassion for all creatures that he not only fed hundreds of dogs, cows, and other animals, he even put food out for the cockroaches. Now that's some serious love.

As I left the Aghori for the last time in the hospital, I asked him, "Aghoriji (*ji* is a term of respect in India), is there anything more that I need to know?"

"You are not your body," he replied. As I traveled throughout India in the following months I thought of this many times as my body was racked with vomiting, diarrhea, and intense headaches. Thank goodness I am not my body!

On a deeper level, I understood that the Aghori was telling me that the reality of my life transcends the physical form of my body. When I let go of the identification with the body, I open myself to the unbounded awareness of pure Self. This is the domain of bliss, of real fulfillment in life.

Passion leads to fulfillment by helping us to become more intimately connected with our deepest nature. That's why we say your passions are the clues to your personal destiny. Ultimately, your destiny is the spontaneous expression of your pure Self expressed through your individual life.

Staying Open

The path of passion takes some interesting twists and turns. It was about to take a big turn for me.

As it came time to leave Nepal, Juliann came to me and said, "Janet, I can't go, I'm sorry."

"What?!" I screeched.

"I can't go. I need to stay in Nepal and find what my passion is."

Shocked would not even begin to describe my state. Juliann was my producer, the expert who knew how to run the camera, work the microphones, and manage the filming. Yet on some deep level I knew this had to be a blessing. Everything always was.

With just a few hours to go before I had to catch my plane to Delhi, Juliann quickly gave me a crash course in the use of the equipment she had bought for me.

Chris and I wrote an e-book about staying open in the midst of change, called *From Sad to Glad*. Now I had the chance to practice. So we said a prayer together, and I got on the plane.

As I traveled from place to place I was told of one great master after another.

Ecstasy

My passion to "spend time with the enlightened" was fulfilled more fully than I could ever have imagined.

In Delhi I heard of a great Saint named Hans Baba. He was known for the fact that when he sang his devotees would enter a trancelike state and have remarkable inner experiences.

I traveled from Vrindavan to Delhi and then back to Vrindavan to be with Hans Baba for about a week.

No one knows where Hans Baba will be at any moment. He goes where the mood strikes him. So I had to ask around until I found out his current location, and then traveled there.

One day when I was with Hans Baba, one of his disciples told me today was a holy day and Hans Baba would be feeding and clothing many Sadhus (holy men) from all over India.

"You should come to the celebration, Janet, there is nothing like it," he said.

Within no time, over two thousand Indian Sadhus in orange and white dhotis filled Hans Baba's ashram. One by one they were given food, an envelope that contained Indian rupees, and a woolen shawl. All gifts from Hans Baba.

After the celebration was over, Hans Baba returned to the main hall and again started his melodious trance-like singing.

As he kept up his intonations, one after another, devotees began to rise and dance, apparently in a state of rapture. Later I asked one of the devotees why people are attracted to Hans Baba, and she replied with one word, "Ecstasy."

Ecstasy works for me!

Love Knows No Bounds

I headed south with my friend Martin to the ashram of a great Saint who has become known throughout the world as the "hugging saint," Mata Amritanandamayi Devi, affectionately known as Amma or Ammachi. She got her nickname because she gives hugs to all who come to see her. She's been known to go twenty-four hours or more, giving her love through hugs to thousands of people at a time.

We arrived at Amma's ashram and were immediately

led upstairs to greet this amazing woman. Amma's presence is quite remarkable. Her impact is felt in the world through the huge donations her nonprofit organizations have received and that are now being used to provide hospitals, orphanages, and all manner of charitable services.

After the tsunami that hit southern India and Sri Lanka in 2004, Amma pledged over $23 million in financial aid to build new housing for those displaced and another $1 million to support aid efforts for the victims of Hurricane Katrina in the United States.

In her ashram, Amma is surrounded by thousands of devotees, and she rules the place with love, firmness, and discipline. Being in her presence is like being in the presence of the divine. There are no words to describe it.

During my visit, I had the rare opportunity to film Amma as she fed two of her pet elephants. She laughed and played, putting cookies in her mouth as the elephants took them gently from her with their huge trunks.

Ammachi's love seems to have no bounds, and there is nothing that is too lowly for her. At various times she will lead the way in cleanup duties or doing the "menial" labor required to maintain the ashram. She is a living example of humility in action, the personification of love.

I'm told it is very unusual these days to have time with Amma. I felt incredibly fortunate to be able to spend a week at the ashram and observe this great Saint in action.

Treat the Guest as God

I went on to Mysore, and after spending a week at the Indus Valley Ayurvedic Centre, one of the most sublime, comfortable, luxurious Ayurvedic resorts you can imagine, I spent another week with a Saint who was about as opposite from Hans Baba as one can imagine.

Swami Krishnamurthy is staying at my house for two months as I write these words. I first met him at his 150-acre organic mango farm about two hours outside Bangalore.

Swamiji is a fountainhead of knowledge. Ask him one question and you will receive a complete description of that aspect of life. It seems there is nothing he does not understand in depth.

I sat mesmerized for hours as he described to me the nature of fulfillment, the experience of being, the meaning of contact with Source, the purpose of life, and the ephemeral nature of the things we in the West call our lives.

After his discourses, Swamiji took me out to greet his cows, tour the mango orchards, pick some grapes, and enjoy the beauty of the land in which he lives.

In India there is an ancient tradition that says one should treat a guest as God. In Swamiji's home I really discovered what that means. His family couldn't be more attentive or more giving of their love.

There was no need I had that wouldn't be fulfilled and no comfort within their ability to provide that they wouldn't offer. It was truly a remarkable experience.

Striking the Bull's-eye

After filming wonderful hours of Swamiji's expositions, I took a flight to Rishikesh in the Himalayas. I stopped in to visit my old friend His Holiness Swami Chidanand Saraswati, affectionately known as Pujya Swamiji. Pujya Swamiji has millions of followers throughout Asia, and his good works are unending. Every evening, thousands gather at his ashram on the banks of the Ganges, overseen by a huge statue of Lord Shiva, for chanting and Vedic ceremonies.

I headed up to Uttarkashi, high in the Himalayas, known as "the Valley of the Saints." This is a place where many are drawn who have chosen to retire from the world for spiritual pursuits. While sitting in a hotel in this tiny town, I had the feeling of being in the presence of another master.

Looking around I saw three Indian men in a corner. I approached them and asked, "Are one of you by chance a guru?" Of course you can only ask such a thing in the rarified air of the high mountains of the Himalayas, but in this environment it seemed quite natural.

One of the men looked very irritated with me, one seemed indifferent, and the third replied, "Madam, you have struck the bull's-eye! This is Pilot Baba (indicating the indifferent man), renowned throughout India."

Later I would discover that Pilot Baba is indeed renowned throughout India and has been filmed as he was submerged in a tank of water for five continuous days. I asked if I could interview him. Pilot Baba smiled and said, "Of course. If it will help the world, why not?!"

As I spent the next few days in the presence of Pilot

Baba, he invited me to go with him and some of his devotees to Gomukh, the source of the holy river Ganges,
which emerges from a glacier high in the Himalayas.

When the Good Is Disguised

Having no clue what I was getting myself into, I immediately said yes. The day we were to begin the long hike,
Pilot Baba decided he would not take the trek and asked
if I would like to stay in Gangotri with him and a few
others. But having heard about the journey to Gomukh,
nothing could make me turn back at this point, not even
more time with the wonderful Pilot Baba.

"It can be a very rough trip," he warned.

"Are you sure you are up for it?" he asked, concerned.

"Absolutely!" I said. "I do yoga!"

It made no difference to me that it was a seven-hour
trek through the high mountains. I paid no attention to
the fact that I only had very thin cotton punjabis to wear
(an Indian dress with cotton pants and a long, dresslike
top). The possibility of visiting this very famous pil-
grimage spot was too irresistible.

I borrowed a cotton jacket, bought myself a wool cap,
socks, and a very thin pair of white tennis shoes, joined
a group of Pilot Baba's devotees from Japan, and off we
went.

Now seven hours of walking is a pretty good outing
for me under the best of circumstances. But this wasn't
just seven hours of walking. This was uphill, in super-
high altitude and half the time clambering over rocks
and huge boulders.

When we left Gangotri the sun was shining with not a cloud in sight.

"A piece of cake," I thought.

Pilot Baba's Japanese contingency snickered as I walked past them in my white cotton punjabis and clean white tennis shoes.

I'll show them what this Hollywood girl is made of!

About two hours into this hike, it started snowing, and I was beginning to shiver. It was okay as long as we kept moving, but when we stopped to rest, I started shaking all over, my head started to ache, and my stomach was in misery. Worst of all, I was becoming extremely emotional and started to cry as I was walking.

Almost to Gomukh we stopped at a government camp to rest overnight. Word of my condition spread to other pilgrims at the camp. Not long after I collapsed on a canvas cot in one of the tents, a doctor from Ahmedabad miraculously showed up. He informed me that I had altitude sickness. It was nothing to worry about, and I just needed to take the pills he left with me.

A little while later a homeopathic doctor arrived, who also left me with some remedies. Then an Indian Sadhu (an ascetic or renunciate) came to my tent, gave me a *tulsi* leaf, and told me to slowly chew on it for its medicinal properties. A kind woman dropped in, who gave me a pair of her brand new blue jeans so I would be warmer. Someone else brought me a warm pair of mittens and socks, and before long I was well bundled up.

It was the most remarkable experience to be thousands of miles from home and be so well taken care of.

This is another valuable lesson. When you follow the path of your passions, you will find support coming from places you could never have imagined. Your job is to do the best you can with what you have and be open to all the good that comes to you from those unexpected places.

Be alert. Sometimes the good coming to you may be disguised as something apparently uncomfortable or undesirable, like my altitude sickness. When this happens, stay open to see where the good is coming within the discomfort.

In spite of all my extra layers, that night it got so cold I insisted that my friend Tapash who was traveling with me, a lifelong celibate and meditation teacher from Rishikesh, get in my sleeping bag, not for any conjugal pleasures, but solely for warmth.

I didn't give him a lot of choice as I told him, "Tapash, if you don't get in my sleeping bag I will freeze to death. Get in *now!*" I can't imagine I would have survived that night otherwise.

The next morning the sun was shining and I felt like a new woman. (Don't you even think that!) As we trekked the final few hours to the source of the Ganges, I was in awe. Tall mountain peaks pierced the sky, ruling this world with their inherent majesty.

Being in this remarkable setting felt like being in another world. The conveniences of modern life are nonexistent and the stark beauty of the surroundings is breathtaking.

Arriving at Gomukh, I joined other pilgrims who came to this place to dip themselves in the frigid waters of the torrent called the Ganges as it emerged from under a giant glacier. Tapash, who had mastered the art of breath control, sat in that water for almost five minutes before I made him get out. For me it was all I could do to wet myself with this holy, yet absolutely freezing water.

My predominant memory from this time is of deep-felt emotions that rose to the surface. The profound spiritual quality of this place brought tears to my eyes. I wish I could find words to describe it, yet it was one of those indescribable moments. To know what I'm talking about, I think you'll just have to come with me next time (bet you're looking forward to that! ☺).

As I climbed over rocks to get a better shot of the emerging Ganges, all of a sudden my foot slipped, and down I fell, tumbling over the boulders only to stop within a foot of the raging waters. Had my fall not been broken at that point, you wouldn't be reading this story right now. It was definitely one of those near-death moments.

With reluctance, I left this mountain cathedral and back at the tent camp found a donkey to carry me the rest of the way home. I fed my donkey some of the treats I had with me, and then as I walked around to his other side he gave me a belting kick! Down on the ground I went. Fortunately, no serious damage was done.

Beauty Beyond Description

I returned to Uttarkashi and stayed for a few days at a gorgeous little guesthouse to recover. I can't begin to describe how sublime this time was. I spent my days by the banks of the Ganges, surrounded by mammoth mountains covered with trees, under a clear blue sky. Spending time in deep meditation, I understood why the holy men chose the Himalayas to realize the divine. Here it was so effortless.

While I was hiking around the Himalayas, I heard of

a revered Saint from England who lived in a small hut by the banks of the river. Just hearing about her purity and love I knew I had to find her.

Nani Ma has spent over thirty years in India. During her time in the Himalayas she spent many months at Gomukh, where I had just been, dipping herself in the freezing waters of the Ganges three times a day as a spiritual purification.

After much coaxing, she finally allowed me to interview her. Now I wasn't sure how this would work, since Nani Ma is not a particularly attractive woman. She was in an auto accident as a child and one eye is half an inch above the other; she hasn't had any dental work for years so her teeth appear to be in dire need of attention; and she has hardly any hair.

However, once she began to speak I started to understand what real beauty is. This remarkable woman spoke with such depth of understanding, and her beautiful heart overflowed so completely, that Nani Ma transformed into a beautiful goddess right before my eyes.

With tears streaming down my face, I could hardly hold the camera. Never had I seen someone so completely transformed.

"Nani Ma," I said, crying. "Thank you so much. You have truly shown me what real beauty is."

Once again I understood why spending time with the enlightened is such a passion for me. This woman is like none I have ever met. She has such a profound understanding of life, her words were so simple yet so illuminating, and she is a living embodiment of love.

Very few people know Nani Ma is present in the world, and yet I have no doubt her silent inward quality of life has as profound an effect on some level as the great boundless activity of Saints like Ammachi or Pujya Swamiji.

Miracles Come in Many Forms

I traveled back to Rishikesh and went to visit my dear friend, a beautiful woman Saint, Devi Vanamali. She and Nani Ma share the same deep inner beauty.

Vanamali welcomed me into her home. I sat for hours transfixed by her profound insights and wisdom. One morning before I was leaving, she told me there was a remarkable healer in Kerala named Sri Sunil Das whom I absolutely had to go see.

This man had been diagnosed with terminal cancer about five years before and had been cured of the disease by Sai Baba (another revered teacher with millions of followers in southern India). With Sunil Das's cure came the ability to cure others, and he had been using this special gift ever since.

Vanamali told me that Sunilji feeds over five thousand local villagers every day, treats more than thirty-five leper families daily, and that leaders from throughout India come to his simple home for healing.

Now under other circumstances I would have been thrilled. But I had already been in India for over three months, and Kerala was in the far south of India, a long trip from Vanamali's home in the Himalayas near Rishikesh.

I put the thought aside and went back to Rishikesh to prepare to return to Delhi the following day.

While I was eating breakfast, Devi Vanamali's cousin Mohan came to say good-bye to me.

"I have a message from Sri Sunil Das," Mohan said excitedly.

"Sri Sunil who?" I asked.

"Sri Sunil Das. The healer that Vanamali told you about yesterday."

"Oh," I said. Unimpressed, I kept chewing my toast and looking out the restaurant window at the beautiful Ganges below.

"He gave me a message for you," Mohan said.

"Uh huh," I said, as I buttered my sixth piece of toast.

"He said to tell you that you have great blessings from three Himalayan masters." He finally got my attention.

"Maharishi, Yogananda, and Babaji," Mohan exclaimed.

Upon hearing those three names I immediately dropped my toast in my lap.

"Who?!" I asked in disbelief.

"Maharishi, Yogananda, and Babaji," Mohan repeated, smiling.

My heart felt like it had stopped beating. Maharishi Mahesh Yogi is the master with whom I have studied for over thirty-six years, Paramahansa Yogananda was the first master I had ever known, and Babaji had lived in my heart ever since I read about him in Yogananda's *Autobiography of a Yogi*.

"Can we call Sunil Das?" I asked.

"Of course!" Mohan said as he grabbed my cell phone, dialed the number, and handed it back to me.

"Hello?"

"*Codi, codi pranam*," a voice said. "You come?"

When I heard that voice I knew there just wasn't an option, so I said yes, I would come. A few days later I arrived at Sunilji's home near Coimbatore in Kerala and was welcomed with open arms.

This man in his early forties struck me with his down-to-earth, playful, fun, and apparently "normal" personality. Yet his humility, innocence, and profound effect on everyone who meets him are undeniable.

I watched as every day thousands of villagers from throughout that area came and were fed from Sunilji's kitchen. I filmed the faces and deformed bodies of lepers who had suffered from this dread disease, in some cases for more than forty years, and who now smiled and laughed.

I sat day after day as people from throughout India came to Sunilji with one ailment or another and received his prayers, his blessings, and the healing that he insists comes from God.

I heard story after story of the miraculous, which seems to follow Sunilji wherever he goes, and I witnessed many, many cases when he manifested sacred ash and gave it to those who visited him to treat their diseases. From statuettes to pearls to pendants to bells, Sunilji was constantly materializing gifts out of thin air.

I can't imagine that these feats were concocted after having watched them so many times, and yet these are not the things that make Sunilji special. That comes from his deep devotion to God. Every moment of his day is committed to service in the name of God. Every healing his visitors experience he credits to God.

He takes no money for himself. All donations go to the charitable trust established to support his work, which is run by a former president of India.

Sunilji showed me what a life of service truly looks like, and it is an amazing thing to witness.

After I had stayed in his home for some time, I learned that my friend Jack Canfield was coming to Bombay. I immediately had the thought, "What can I do to make Jack's visit to India extra special?"

I made some arrangements and then flew to Bombay to meet Jack when he arrived. I met him at his hotel and discovered that his bags had never arrived from the United States. So we spent our first few hours together in one of my favorite activities—shopping!

It turned out Pujya Swamiji and Sadhvi Bhagwati Saraswati from Rishikesh were in Bombay at that time, as were my friends Catherine Oxenberg (well-known actress and princess of Yugoslavia) and her actor husband Casper van Dien (*Starship Troopers, Sleepy Hollow, The Omega Code, Tarzan,* and others). I made arrangements with Pankaj and Smita Naram for us all to have dinner together the night before Jack's seminar.

Was that an amazing evening! Imagine having dinner with two Saints, one of the bestselling authors in the world, two world-famous Ayurvedic physicians, and two famous movie actors. It was definitely one of those memorable moments.

I spent the next few days with Catherine and Casper in their suite at one of Bombay's finest hotels. During those days it happened that Sunilji was also in Bombay, asked to come by one of his famous devotees.

I took Sunilji to the airport as he was leaving Bombay and got a call from a dear Indian friend who is very well respected in that city, sitting on the boards of more than twenty-five educational institutions. I had introduced her to Sri Sunil Das the day before. One of her oldest and dearest friends was in the hospital and appeared to be dying. She was deeply distressed and asked if Sunilji could come.

"Oh Maya, I'm so sorry. Sunil Das just got a call from the royal family in Kerala and they need him to come right now. I'm so sorry," I told her.

As I hung up the phone, Sunil Das said, "Janet go!"

"Huh?" I stammered.

"You go!" he said.

"Sunilji, what can I do? I'm not a healer!" I said.

With those words, Sunil Das immediately manifested from thin air the gray ash known as *vibhuti*, or healing ash.

Handing the ash to me, Sunil Das said, "You must go immediately; do not stop, go immediately." He then instructed me to put the sacred ash into the dying woman's mouth.

With that, off I went. Although I was sorely tempted to stop along the way at some of the great shops I had planned to be visiting that day, Sunilji clearly told me to go immediately, so on I went.

When I walked into the room I was surprised to find a young girl sitting on the bed of the dying woman with her head on the woman's stomach. The girl immediately looked up at me and said, "Oh Janet, I'm so glad you are here! My mother is dying."

These words came from Premala, another of my dear Indian friends. As it turned out it was Premala's mother who was dying (a fact I hadn't known until that moment).

I took Premala's hand, put the ash in her mother's mouth as Sunil had instructed, then began singing the

Mrityunjaya Mantra, a special chant I had been taught for those who are sick or dying or in need of protection. Within a few minutes of my arrival, Premala's mother took three deep breaths and passed away.

Aware of a beautiful light that was flooding the room, I said to my friend who was now sobbing uncontrollably, "Premala, can you feel how happy your mother is?" With those words Premala stopped crying. "Can you feel how light it is in the room, Premala?" I asked.

"I can," she said, as her eyes grew wide with wonder.

"I can!" she said again, and started smiling and laughing all at the same time.

Later Premala told me my coming to the hospital had been a true lifesaver for her. After my arrival and taking the sacred ash from Sunilji, she felt her mother had been truly blessed. The deep grief she had been feeling lifted and she felt a great relief.

This is one of several experiences that caused my respect for Sunilji to deepen to a profound level. Somehow, he had known it was urgent that I go immediately to the hospital and as a result, a profound effect occurred.

When Your Passions Start Coming to You

I have been back from India for several months now. After spending months traveling throughout India and Nepal meeting the most remarkable individuals I have ever encountered, my passion to spend time with the enlightened continues to be fulfilled, over and over again.

Since returning home, my Saintly friends have been coming to me. A few weeks after my return, Hariprasad Swamiji, a master whose birthday I'd attended along with eighty thousand other people, came to my home to visit. A few days later, five of his female renunciates called Benus came and stayed for several days, filling my house with laughter and love. Then not long after, my dear Bapuji came for a couple of days, and the profound Swami Krishnamurthy, at whose home I had been treated with such kindness, is now here for two months.

My life has become a series of miracles. In my upcoming book *The Saints Speak Out*, I'll share all the details of this remarkable trip, but hopefully you have a taste of why I called this the best experience of my life.

Trekking to the source of the Ganges, discovering that fire can be a blessing, witnessing the effects of Sunilji's apparently miraculous healings, listening to Swami Krishnamurthy's profound discourses, these experiences were amazing. Then experiencing divine love in the presence of Ammachi, Bapuji, Hans Baba, Hariprasad Swamiji, Nani Ma, Devi Vanamali, and all of the other Saints I was blessed to meet completely blew me away. Add to that all the other remarkable events on this incredible journey. This is what made my trip to India the most transforming experience of my life. And those experiences weren't the whole of it.

It was also the best and most amazing experience because I learned what is truly possible when you allow yourself to give in fully to going for what you love. I learned that money will show up when and as it is needed. I learned how important it is to let go of one's own concepts of how one's passions will get fulfilled and to stay open to the ways life is appearing. I learned that the obstacles and challenges along the way simply don't matter when you feel the fire of passion inside—with that fire nothing can stop you.

Perhaps most importantly, I learned once again that God is good and God is everything. When I am willing to let go of my will and open to God's will, meaning the way life is unfolding, then life becomes an incredible adventure and consistently fulfilling.

The Power of Passion

"How was your trip?" Chris asked.

"It was absolutely the best and most amazing experience of my entire life," Janet replied.

What will the best and most amazing experience of your life look like? By now we hope you understand that you have the power to craft that experience.

You are creating your life and your world in every moment. Want to see how powerful you are? Look at your life.

Your life today is the result of the predominant thoughts you have held up until now. If you want your life to change, change your mind. It doesn't have to take a long time.

What will you put your attention on now? What did you learn from Janet's story?

Here are a few of the things we hope you picked up:

- Your life won't look the way you think it will.
- Get clear on the "what" and the "how" will begin to appear.
- Your challenge is to stay open, let go of your concepts

about how your life should be, and embrace the way it is.

- You will know you are aligned with your passions when things happen to you that others might find uncomfortable, distasteful, or undesirable, and they don't even faze you because you are so driven by the fire inside.

- Be prepared to find blessings coming to you from situations and circumstances that may at first appear to be the opposite (e.g., Janet's stepmother passing away or her altitude sickness in the Himalayas). Learn to look for the blessing.

- It takes courage to follow your own path. Surround yourself with people who support you in following your dreams. Avoid spending time with people who try to destroy them.

- Passion is a journey, not a destination. Every day choose in favor of your top passions and you will soon find yourself living a passionate life.

- When you love the process, the results will take care of themselves.

- Life is here to enjoy. The purpose of life is the expansion of happiness. When it appears otherwise, you are off the path of destiny. Look at your life and ask, "What do I need to change to choose in favor of my passions?"

Passion has the power to transform your life. When you discover your deepest passions, you connect with the essence of who you are. Living life aligned with your passions, your personal destiny unfolds naturally and effortlessly.

When that happens, life becomes an expanding field of joy, happiness, and fulfillment, along with all the same inconve-

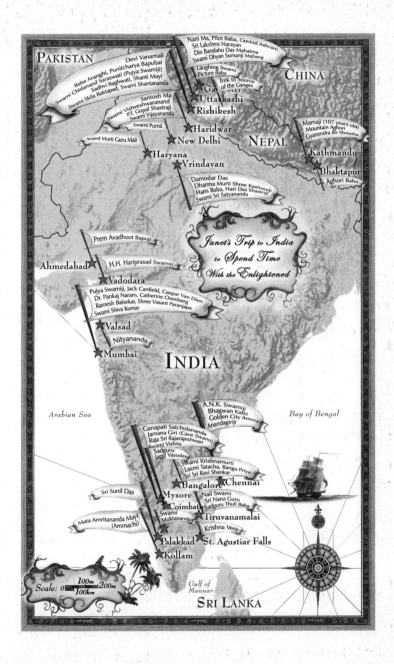

PAKISTAN

Devi Vanamali
Baba Aranghi, Punitcharya Bapubai
Swami Chidanand Saraswati (Pujya Swamiji)
Sadhvi Bagbwati, Shanti Mayi
Swami Skila Baktapad, Swami Shantananda

Nani Ma, Pilot Baba, Govind Ashram
Sri Lakshmi Narayan
Din Bandahu Das Mahatma
Swami Dhyan Sumanji Maharaj

CHINA

Laughing Swami
Picture Baba

Trek to Source
of the Ganges

Santosh Ma
Swami Vishveshwaranand
P.T. Gopal Shastraji
Swami Vijayananda

★ Gangotri

★ Uttarkashi
★ Rishikesh

Swami Purna

★ Haridwar

Anand Murti Guru Maa

★ New Delhi

NEPAL

Mamaji (107 years old)
Mountain Aghori
Gyanendra Bir Shrestha

★ Haryana

★ Kathmandu

★ Vrindavan

★ Bhaktapur

Aghori Baba

Damodar Das
Dharma Murti Shree Kashoreji
Hans Baba, Hari Das Shastriji
Swami Sri Satyananda

Prem Avadhoot Bapuji

Janet's Trip to India
to Spend Time
With the Enlightened

H.H. Hariprasad Swamiji

Ahmedabad ★

★ Vadodara

Pujya Swamiji, Jack Canfield, Caspar Van Dien
Dr. Pankaj Naram, Catherine Oxenberg
Ramesh Balsekar, Shree Vasant Paranjape
Swami Shiva Kumar

★ Valsad

Nityananda

★ Mumbai

INDIA

Arabian Sea

Bay of Bengal

A.N.K. Swamiji
Bhagwan Kalki
Golden City Amma
Anandagiriji

Ganapati Satchidananda
Jamana Giri (Cave Swami)
Raja Sri Rajarajeshwari
Swami Vishnu
Sadguru
Jaggi Vasudev

Swami Krishnamurti
Laxmi Tatacha, Ranga Priya
Sri Sri Ravi Shankar

Sri Sunil Das

★ Bangalore ★ Chennai

★ Mysore

Nail Swami
Sri Nana Guru
Sadguru Thuli Baba

Mata Amritananda Mayi
(Ammachi)

★ Coimbate

Swami
Muktananda

★ Tiruvanamalai

Krishna Vera

★ Palakkad ★ St. Agustiar Falls

★ Kollam

Gulf of
Mannar

Scale: 0 100m 200m
         100km

SRI LANKA

niences, challenges, obstacles, and discomforts everyone experiences. The difference is, on the path of passion, those things
just don't have much significance.

In the previous pages we've given you tools to create greater
and greater clarity about your passions and the things that are
most meaningful to you. Have we told you enough times how
important clarity is to create the life of your dreams?

Now that you have the tools, we are going to share with
you the experiences, wisdom, and sage advice of masters of
transformation from the East and the West. Benjamin Franklin had this to say about gaining wisdom:

> **There are two ways to acquire wisdom; you can
> either buy it or borrow it. By buying it, you pay full
> price in terms of time and cost to learn the lessons
> you need to learn. By borrowing it, you go to those
> men and women who have already paid the price to
> learn the lessons and get their wisdom from them.**

When you borrow the wisdom of those who have already paid
the price, you can shortcut the path to fulfilling your own destiny. In the second half of this book, we will introduce you to
the essential tools for following the cosmic highway to fulfilling your destiny.

We'll also share with you interviews we've conducted with
some of the most remarkable people in the world, so you can
borrow their wisdom for living a passionate life. Every good
meal requires proper seasoning, so we'll spice up part 2 with
some of the stories of everyday people who have made The
Passion Test a part of their lives—and what has happened as a
result.

PART TWO

Traveling the Cosmic Highway: Creating the Life You Choose to Live

You are only as powerful as your mentors.
—*Mark Victor Hansen and Robert G. Allen*

WHAT YOU THINK
YOU BECOME

It is the combination of thought
and love which forms the irresistible force
of the law of attraction.

—*Charles Haanel*

D o you remember our friend Bill Levacy's formula
for creating the life you choose to live?

Intention—Attention—No Tension

Okay. You've covered the intention part by clarifying your passions. You've committed to aligning your life with those passions. You have created a clear picture of what your passionate life will look like. In fact, you've looked back from the vantage point of your 100th birthday, and it's a pretty wonderful life, isn't it? (See how much faith we have in what you've already done?)

The entire first half of this book was to help you get clear on your intentions. What do you really choose to create in your life?

So, what's next? Attention.

Much has been written and discussed lately about "the law of attraction" a.k.a. The Secret. The Secret is all about attention. You draw into your life what you give attention to. When you put your attention on what brings you joy, happiness, and fulfillment, you get more of it. When you put your attention on what's wrong with things in the world around you, on all the reasons there are to be dissatisfied, then you get more dissatisfaction.

We asked some of the Saints Janet interviewed in India about this powerful principle. They gave us some surprising and thought-provoking answers. In a moment we'll share some of those, but, first, Chris tells how we first heard about The Secret.

> Janet was traveling in India on June 27, 2005, when I was contacted by a subscriber to *Healthy Wealthy nWise* named Rhonda Byrne. When I heard this name I thought it sounded familiar, and then I remembered she had enrolled in our Alliance Secrets program, in which we teach how to create "enlightened alliances."
>
> Today millions of people around the world know Rhonda Byrne as the creator of the movie and book phenomenon called *The Secret*. Yet when Rhonda contacted us, she was just like any other ordinary person. She wasn't famous. She had gone through some very rough times not long before. She had a dream. She had

skills and talents. She was passionate about her dream, and she began to take action.

I talked with our partners at *Healthy Wealthy nWise*, Ric and Liz Thompson. As it turned out, Rhonda had contacted them as well. We all agreed it was worth talking to Rhonda, so I called her.

"Oh Chris, I'm so pleased you called! I love The Passion Test. In fact, I've had every one of my staff take it. It's phenomenal!"

It was impossible not to be attracted to the exuberant, loving voice on the other end of the phone. With excitement, Rhonda explained how she was using The Secret to create *The Secret*.

She told the story of creating a series of trailers and sending them to the top executives at the largest television networks in Australia. When she invited them to fly in and hear "the Secret revealed" at her studio, all of them did—something that was unheard of in her industry. The Nine Network, the largest TV network in Australia, won the bidding and agreed to air *The Secret*. Now, she had just arrived in the United States and would soon begin filming.

After talking with her, Rhonda's message resonated deeply. We agreed to connect again when I could get Janet on the phone from India.

We did that a few days later and after talking with her, both Janet and I agreed that we would do whatever we could to support Rhonda's project. Her vision was huge, and her ability to create a sense of mystery and excitement was remarkable.

Her most important need was to arrange interviews with teachers who understood the principles her film was going to present. We also told her that our partners, Liz and Ric, would be happy to help with the technical aspects of getting a website set up, and she was thrilled.

Janet and I both got on the phone (Janet making calls from India 12½ hours away) and started lining up teachers for Rhonda's film, many of whom we had interviewed for the *Healthy Wealthy nWise* Passion series.

Two months later, we had attracted thirty-six of the fifty-two interviews Rhonda and her team completed for *The Secret*. It is a testimony to Rhonda's vision and her deep understanding of the principles she presented that as of this writing, over 3.75 million copies of the book *The Secret* are in print, and over 2 million people have purchased the DVD or viewed the online version.

What made *The Secret* so successful was the power of Rhonda's attention. She consistently and constantly gave attention to the things she was choosing to create. When the inevitable challenges came up, she didn't dwell on them. She gave attention to the things she loved in her life and that gave her a sense of joy.

The Secret is based on the principle we have shared with you throughout this book:

**What you put your attention on
grows stronger in your life.**

When you are presented with anything, give attention to the ideas, the principles, and the concepts that resonate with you and that will serve you in improving your life. Put them into practice. Learn from your own experience.

When you hear people criticizing, berating, or finding fault with something or someone dear to you, you have a choice. You can focus on how wrong they are. You can put your attention on the negative things they are saying. Or you can ask yourself: How can I use this information to gain greater clarity? Where is the gift in this?

Using attention to attract what you choose to have in your life can create practical, valuable changes in your relationships with anyone, and particularly with those you love and care about. Janet tells this story:

A few months before they were supposed to get married, a good friend came to me, worried about her fiancé.

"Peter doesn't have a clue about how to manage money, and I'm afraid if I put my hard-earned savings in with his, in no time it will all be gone, and that scares the hell out of me," Jody confided.

She went on, "He's an impulse buyer, and he spends his money on anything and everything. At the end of the month when the bills are due, he doesn't have enough money to handle his commitments. I love him so much," she said, with tears in her eyes. "And I just don't know if I can live with the way he deals with money."

It hurt to see Jody so distressed, and yet Peter was also a good friend of mine. The last thing I wanted was to get in the middle of their personal life. I decided the best thing to do as Jody's friend was to be a good listener as she shared her story.

After about half an hour, Jody said she felt better just

getting to talk to someone, and she was so happy that I didn't give her advice.

"Thanks so much for being there for me, Janet. I'm going to go home and think about the answer," she said. "I just know if I ask inside for direction the answer will come. It always does."

About three months later Jody called me, excitedly saying she had some wonderful news to share. When we met she had a glow around her I had never seen before.

"Well, what's the good news?" I asked, thrilled to see Jody smiling from ear to ear.

"Peter has made a 100 percent turnaround with money!" she blurted out.

"Wow, Jody, that's so great! How did that happen so quickly?" I asked.

"Well, I kept thinking about how I could support Peter with this money issue, without making him feel I was being critical of him. Finally, one day the answer just came. I decided that instead of following in the path of Peter's last wife and nagging him to death about how he handled money, I was going to do just the opposite. I would look for opportunities when I could honestly and truthfully tell him how fabulous he was at handling our finances.

"So, whenever he did something responsible and well planned with money, I made a big fuss over him and told him how wonderful it was to be with a man who could really take care of me. At first he couldn't quite believe it, but as I continued doing this over and over, it got to the point that every time I did, Peter's face would light up, and I swear Janet, he'd grow an inch every time."

"That is so completely amazing, Jody. Good for you!" I told her. "Can I ask you a question?"

"Sure," she said.

"What did you do when he blew it with your money? I mean, he didn't just change overnight, did he? How did you handle that?" I asked, hardly able to wait for Jody's answer.

She looked me straight in the eyes and said, "I just shut up. As hard as it was for me, I didn't say a word. I just shut up.

"Let me tell you, Janet, shutting up was one of the hardest things I have ever done. There were times when I thought I was going to go crazy from not being able to scream at him for being so careless and thoughtless. Yet when I held myself back from nagging him, which I always would have done in the past, I won in spades every time. Peter was happier, I was happier, everyone was happier!

"So, the biggest win for me was not only that Peter make a 100 percent turnaround in the way he handles money, but I made a 100 percent turnaround in where I put my attention, which really raised my happiness quotient off the scales. And the biggest win of all . . . Peter and I have been like two little love birds ever since, and we're getting married as planned. You'll come, won't you?"

"I wouldn't miss it for the world, Jody."

When you realize that every single thing you experience in life has some benefit to offer you, you'll discover that there is no longer anything to fight against or to be defensive about. Not only that, you will discover that people, situations, and re-sources are drawn to you in ways you could never have pre-dicted. This is when life becomes magical.

Let's take it to a deeper level. Do you remember Nani Ma, the beautiful Saint Janet discovered living on the banks of the Ganges River, high in the Himalayas? She has spent the past thirty-five years hidden away in the mountains, devoting her life to the experience of truth. Here is what Nani Ma said about the law of attraction and some of the other ideas we've shared with you.

Nani Ma

I (Janet) first came to know about Nani Ma through my wonderful friend Krishna. About two to three times a year Krishna travels to India for the sole purpose of hang-ing out with enlightened Saints. When I asked him who he felt I had to meet, Nani Ma was way up on the top of his list.

This was quite a recommendation as I knew Krishna had met many enlightened souls. He was very careful about sharing them with anyone until he felt they were the "real deal" and were truly awake.

My first reaction to Nani Ma was surprise. She is from England, not India as I had presumed.

It only took a few minutes of connecting with her be-fore I knew why Krishna had sent me to her. Nani Ma has that amazing and distinctive glow I have come to appreciate in the enlightened masters with whom I've visited.

Living a life of total service, absorbed in the study of deep meditation and austerities, Nani Ma has become the embodiment of pure knowledge and love. When I began working on this new edition of The Passion Test, *I asked her to talk about the law of attraction and how one can create a wonderful life. Her answers were profound:*

"The way to create whatever you want in life is by giving it to other people. Sometimes people think they want money or a husband or children, but nobody really wants anything except happiness. The pursuit of all these other things is only for the sake of happiness.

"The way to have happiness is to give what you want to have. On the relative plane, life is just like a mirror. Whatever you do, that is what you will receive.

"So if you want to receive happiness then you must give happiness. If you want to receive love then you must give love. If you want to receive respect then you must give respect.

"To receive love, to be happy and successful in life, we have to be open. We have to open our hearts, open ourselves. If we just open ourselves, everything will flow to us.

"And to attract what you want in your life, to use the law of attraction, you must be completely committed. One must be committed to what one wants, and what one wants is love and happiness. So one must be committed to giving those things, to being harmonious in life in God's creation.

"If someone is not committed then they become confused. They become spread out. We know that if anything is concentrated, whatever it may be, that is where power comes. If we are spread out, then there is no power and everything just blows away. If you want something to be strong, if you want something to be sure, something to work, you have to be committed."

As I was talking with Nani Ma I wanted to know why so many people feel such a strong impulse to serve as they get aligned with their passions. In my own life I have found myself drawn to working with homeless women and supporting projects for juvenile offenders. In business, success only comes when you truly serve your customers. I asked Nani Ma why this aspect of providing service seems so important when you are living your passions. Here's what she said:

"When we serve other people we forget ourselves, we go out of ourselves. And the misery of life is when we are lost in ourselves, meaning in our egos. When we serve other people we tend to forget our little personalities for a while. I t is our little personalities that bring us misery. When we serve other people we go out of ourselves. And then we shine inside, God shines, our true nature shines, and that is happiness.

"For some enlightened people, their hearts are already open. They are already without the ego. These people are already in bliss. Those people who are happy in themselves serve because there is nothing else to do.

"They feel compassion. They are already close to God. There is nothing left to attain in their life, but they have a body, so they use it to help others, to help other people that haven't understood that God is everywhere. To help people who don't have joy in their lives and who have pain. It is natural that the enlightened want to help them out of their sorrow. For the enlightened it is totally natural because they already have everything in life."

As my time with Nani Ma drew to a close, I wanted to know the relationship between the law of attraction and the understanding that life is unified at its core.

"When we forget our little selves and start to love others then we receive love, which is what we want. When we receive and give love, we understand brotherhood. And when we go deeper into brotherhood, it becomes unity.

"We all need the same things and we all want the same things. So this law of attraction is based on love. I'm not talking about attracting worldly things but attracting what humans really want, what humans really need, which is to be in harmony and to be one with one another.

"Other things are so superficial. They are just like little sticks floating on a deep river. But the deep river is the love and harmony that we feel between each other and which is directly related to our oneness. The deeper we go, the nearer we come to unity. Only when we are far out on the surface do we want all these little things, and we don't understand what it is that we really want.

"When we think that we want this or we want that, we should go more deeply and find out what we really want. Then we will discover that what we really want is just happiness and love. In order to find that, we must give it, and then when we give it we break down the barriers that separate people. When we do that, we find there is only unity and there isn't anything else."

RESIGNING AS GENERAL
MANAGER OF THE
UNIVERSE

When we have done all we can do,
remarkable things happen when we surrender.
—*Debbie Ford*

While we were partners with Bob Allen and Mark Victor Hansen, we met Karen Nelson Bell and her husband, Duncan. At that time they had been part of Bob's protégé program for over a year. They were bright, turned on, and upbeat. It was such fun being around them.

At one of Bob's presentations, he asked Karen and Duncan to tell their story. It turns out they had left their six-figure incomes producing award-winning TV and live music shows when there was a downturn in their industry.

A few months later they enrolled in Bob's program. While most of the students were trying to absorb the knowledge they were gaining, Karen and Duncan went out every week and started acting on what they were being taught.

"We didn't have a clue what we were doing, but we were determined to get started," Karen shared. "We bumbled along for four months, but somehow we managed to accumulate more than $1 million worth of properties. Now, a year later, I'm happy to report that our net worth is over $1 million from our real estate properties alone, and the cash flow from those properties is covering our very comfortable lifestyle."

Duncan passed away in 2005, and in spite of losing the love of her life, Karen is a model of the principles we've been teaching. She is actively involved with life, has released a bestselling book, *Nothing Down for Women*, and is living life as she has since we've known her, with passion.

Karen has given the greatest possible tribute to the man she loved by putting her attention on all the blessings in her life, at the same time that she honors his memory.

Attention is about taking action. Karen and Duncan were unique because they took action even before they completely knew what they were doing. When Duncan passed away, Karen continued to take action as she gave attention to those things that enrich her life.

"Intention—Attention—No Tension" does not mean sitting around daydreaming about your intentions. Traveling the cosmic highway requires movement. You begin taking the action that you can see to take right now, just as Karen and Duncan did.

For you maybe it begins with making a list of what you can do to start living your passions. If you're stuck on what action to take, do this.

From Passion to Action

Make a list of all the possible actions you can take that could allow you to begin aligning with your passions and your Markers. If you can do this with some close friends, you'll find it's even more fun to brainstorm in a group.

When you've come up with everything you can think of, use a process similar to The Passion Test. Compare each item on the list to every other item.

Unlike The Passion Test, in which you asked, "Which is more important, this or this?" for this process you will ask a different question. The important issue at this point is to get clear on what you should do first. So you're going to ask the question, "Which would I do first, this or this?"

As you did with The Passion Test, whichever item you select, continue down the list, comparing that item to all the others, until you find a different one that you would do first. Then that becomes the one you compare against the rest of the list.

For example, what if your passion is, "To have a deep, rewarding, mutually respectful relationship with my children" and your list of actions is:

1. Focus on my children's interests and their needs
2. Take the entire family on an incredible adventure
3. Create a college fund for each child
4. Be available to my children when they need support
5. Spend time weekly with each child

The first question is, "Which would I do first, focus on my children's interests and their needs or take the entire family on an incredible adventure?" Perhaps you would answer 1, "Focus on my children's interests."

Now ask, "Which would I do first, focus on my children's interests or create a college fund for each child?" Perhaps again you choose 1. Then you ask, "Which would I do first, focus on my children's interests or be available to my children when they need support?" Now perhaps you would choose 4, "Be available to my children when they need support."

Number 4 then becomes the one you compare to the next item on the list, so your next question is, "Which would I do first, be available to my children when they need support or spend time weekly with each child?" Perhaps you still say, "Be available to my children when they need support." (By the way, there are no right or wrong answers. The answers should be what feels right to you.) Then "Be available to my children when they need support" is your number one action step on this list.

In this example, did you notice that once we had selected 4, we no longer needed to compare 4 to 2 or 3? Just as in The Passion Test, when you select a new item you don't have to go back and compare it to all those that came before.

To complete this exercise, go through your entire list four more times until you have identified the five action steps that are most immediate. Then, for each action step write out a plan for putting that action into effect. This could be a list of steps to take, or it could be writing a page of what you need to do to begin implementing that action.

Nature's Guidance System

By taking action, you are directing your attention to the fulfillment of your passions. Action keeps attention engaged. This is a critical point, so we'll say it again:

Action keeps attention engaged.

It's not action that creates the desired result (even though it may appear that way). It is your intention directed through the process of attention that creates the result. You can see this is true because in almost every case the way in which a result happens is different from the plan of action created for achieving that result.

If your plan of action were creating the result then everything would happen exactly as you planned. Your plan of action keeps your attention engaged in the fulfillment of your intention, and what makes life fun is seeing how the fulfillment will show up.

This is why it is so important to stay open. We can pretty well guarantee that things won't unfold the way you think they will. To give you a tangible example of that is one of the reasons we shared the story of Janet's adventure in part 1. Here's some really, really good news:

**Nature will guide you every step of the way
when you listen to her messages.**

Believe it or not, life is set up to keep you on the cosmic highway to ever increasing joy and fulfillment. Unfortunately, most people today are like the little toy cars that get off the track, hit a wall, and keep spinning their wheels, trying to go through the wall instead of turning and getting back on the track.

Nature guides us through our internal experience of contraction and expansion. To help you picture what we're talking about, get a blank piece of paper. In the top left corner label it "Nature's Guidance System" and draw a vertical line (up and down) in the middle of the paper. At the top of the line write "Joy and Fulfillment." At the bottom write "Misery and Suffering." To the right of the line draw an arrow pointing up, and next to that write "Expansion." To the left of the line draw another arrow pointing down, and next to that write "Contraction."

You know what it feels like when you're contracted, right? Upset, angry, anxious, tense, irritable, shut down, disconnected, unhappy, depressed. Generally, contraction feels uncomfortable.

And you know what it feels like when you're expanded, don't you? Happy, turned on, excited, ready for anything, open, connected, loving, generous, kind, compassionate. All those wonderful things that feel so good.

Now on your piece of paper, make a green light by the word "Expansion" and a red light by the word "Contraction." If you don't have colored pens, draw an open circle with rays coming out for "Expansion" and a filled-in circle for "Contraction."

When you feel expanded, this is Nature's way of telling you to go forward, take action, you're on the right track. When you feel contracted, the cosmic Guidance System is saying, stop, take a break, look again, reflect.

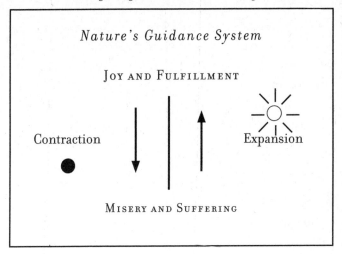

Because contraction is sometimes pretty intense, in *From Sad to Glad* we describe the Expansion Process for dealing with emotional contraction in a constructive way. But for now, just know that when you feel contracted, this is Nature's way of saying, "Take it easy, be kind to yourself, step back and take another look."

Remember "Intention—Attention—No Tension"? This is about No Tension. When you feel contracted and you keep going anyway, when you're feeling exhausted or constricted or uptight and you keep going anyway, you are insisting on your will and not listening to God's will.

When you do that, you are like the toy car. You've rammed into a wall, and you keep spinning your wheels, trying to go through the wall instead of turning, getting back on the track, and speeding forward.

How many times have you thought, "Well, I've got to get this done, it's essential to accomplishing my purpose," so you keep going in spite of the contraction? Or maybe you hit the wall—you just give up and say, "I'll never accomplish my purpose." Guess what? As long as you tell yourself that, it will be true for you. You have turned off the cosmic guidance system.

As long as you keep doing these things you will be moving down and down the line on your paper toward increasing misery and suffering.

When you feel contracted, stop, take a break, and stay open to what is appearing in your life now. You'll be giving yourself the chance for new ideas, new solutions, and new opportunities to show up.

How many stories have we heard of CEOs or inventors or artists or musicians feeling stuck? They were faced with a problem or a challenge and so they took time off from the problem. Maybe they played tennis or went to sleep or took a walk. Then, when they weren't even thinking about the problem, a lightbulb went off and the solution or inspiration appeared to them.

This is the principle of No Tension. When contraction strikes, take a break. Don't try to deal with the challenge in that moment. Some part of your mind will continue to consider the issue, even when you're not consciously thinking about it. And then, when you least expect it, a thought or an idea will come that gives rise to the feeling of expansion again.

It's that *aha* moment, and suddenly you feel excited and turned on again. Expansion is the green light. It's the signal to move forward to take action.

It's really so very simple. The cosmic guidance system is always guiding you as long as you are open to being guided. There are only two states: stop and go. When you feel contraction, stop and look. When you feel expanded, go forward with gusto.

Traveling the cosmic highway to fulfill your destiny has a lot to do with learning to trust that the universe is created to support you in experiencing ever-increasing joy and fulfillment. It means, "resigning as general manager of the universe," as Debbie Ford says. It means letting go of the idea that you have to control everything that happens in your world.

The following Passion interview with Debbie provides some profound points about living your life with openness and awareness.

Debbie Ford

Debbie Ford is the #1 New York Times *bestselling author of* The Dark Side of the Light Chasers: Reclaiming Your Power, Creativity, Brilliance, and Dreams *and an internationally recognized expert in the field of personal transformation and human potential. She is the founder of the Ford Institute for Integrative Coaching at John F. Kennedy University, a personal development organization that provides professional training for individuals committed to leading extraordinary lives. Her teachings and revolutionary inner processes have made her a renowned coach, transformational speaker, and seminar leader.*

"My passion is to teach people to love themselves completely. Not just love the part of themselves that is lovable, like the charming, sweet, smart part, but to love all of themselves, including their darkness.

"I wrote my first book out of this passion to share the idea that God did create us as amazing individuals, and that we all have this similar blueprint within all of us. We all are everything: the good and the bad, the light and the dark, the sweet and the sour, the fearful and the courageous.

"We can't wish the bad parts away, but we can learn to integrate them and love even those parts of ourselves.

"I always try to teach people that there is only so much effort you can put into the world. I remember when *The Dark Side of the Light Chasers* first came out, I was sure it would go to the top of the list. I was going to get on *Oprah* and everything was going to be great and easy.

"I passionately went out in the world and spoke to three people or seven people or fifteen, whoever would listen to me, and it really took years for all the pieces to fit together. I had great people giving Oprah my book, but still nobody called.

"Now I look back and say some things are just meant to be. They're going to happen when they are meant to happen. There is only so much you can accomplish by effort.

"It was at a time when I was surrendering and said, 'Okay, what do I have to do to get my work out into the world? I'll do anything.' I was working day and night to do whatever I had to do. Then, of course, a few things happened. I met Cheryl Richardson, who was on *Oprah* all the time at that point, and she said to me, 'Wow! Your work is so important. What can I do to support you? Why haven't you been on *Oprah*?'

"It was interesting because she had me look at why I hadn't gotten my work out in the world the way I wanted to. What I saw was that I was scared I would become overwhelmed because I was already overwhelmed with my task.

"The moment of truth was seeing that I was the one that had the blocks up. I was the one that was really scared and saying, 'I can't take more than I have.' It reminded me that I didn't really need to do anything. If I would just surrender, God, or my spirit, would take care of me.

"When we have done all we can do, remarkable things happen when we surrender. I did that and literally three days later I got called to do the *Oprah* show. I did three shows and then they reaired all three of them. Within a couple of months my books—and shadow work—went out in the world.

"Our natural instinct is to make things happen and to believe we can do everything, that we are the driver. When you give up being the driver, there is a bigger driver that is going to do a much better job than you. Remember to ask yourself, 'What can I do today to resign as general manager of the universe so I can allow what I am supposed to be doing?'

"I fell in love with a prayer when I was recovering from drug addiction twenty-five years ago. It was in the Alcoholics Anonymous *Big Book*: 'I offer myself to thee to build with me and do with me as thy will. Relieve me of the bondage of self so I may better do thy will.'

"I used to be on my hands and knees every day for five years; my prayer was to just use me, relieve me of what I think I should be doing and allow the universe to use me for some greater cause. I feel like today I am being used for that greater cause, and I love it.

"My recent book *The Best Year of Your Life* is really about becoming the person you desire to be at the end of each year. Not that you have to accomplish a set of external goals, because, yes, I have had many years where I have attained everything I ever wanted in the material world but was left feeling empty inside. The goal is to find balance between inner and outer; at the end of the year, if I have made good choices, if I have allowed myself to evolve, and if I've surrendered and I love who I am then nothing else really matters. That is what I see from teaching and being a trainer and training coaches. When you are loving your life, magic happens.

"*The Best Year of Your Life* is subtitled *Dream It, Plan It, Live It,* and it does give people tools to make things happen in the outer world. But ultimately, its point is, 'Who do I have to be in the inner world to create effortlessly and easily with joy, the things that will nourish me in the outer world?'

"Most people hold a lot of grudges and resentments, not only toward other people, but toward themselves. That unforgiving nature most humans have is a reflection of the internal world where we're beating ourselves up. The way we see the external world is always a mirror of our internal world.

"People internally are beating themselves up, and then all of a sudden they wonder why they're doing things in the outer world to beat themselves up. It's just a way to affirm those internal messages most of us have that we're not good enough or we'll never get what we want, or whatever our programming is.

"To stop sabotaging ourselves, we begin by forgiving ourselves for being part of the human race, with flaws and imperfections, misbehaving and sometimes making wrong choices. We have to forgive ourselves for being flawed, for being imperfect, for not doing it right, for not always behaving, for making choices that are not in our highest and best interests.

"The foundation of all my long-term training is self-forgiveness because what I know is if you can forgive yourself internally and have compassion and openheartedness toward that sweet, vulnerable child who lives inside you, then you will create those kinds of magical moments in the outer world. The outer world will reflect that self-love, and you won't want to sabotage yourself. You'll be careful who you hang around and what you say you're going to do, because you become precious to yourself.

"I love the analogy that we're like these great pieces of art. A sculptor would look at a piece of stone, and they can see the magnificence in it. They know what the creation is, so all they have to do is chisel away anything that's not it, and there they are. They have a masterpiece.

"That's all we have to do. We don't have to become anything, we already are everything we ever wanted to be, and we just have to chisel away anything that is distracting us or blocking us from seeing that self. Then, voilà—we wind up in our power naturally."

What were the key lessons from this interview about living your passion?

1. We all have dark aspects, parts of ourselves we feel ashamed of, scared of, or embarrassed by. We can't wish those parts away, but we can learn to integrate them and love even those parts of ourselves.

2. Some things are meant to be, and they're going to happen when they are meant to be. There is only so much you can accomplish through effort.

3. When we have done all we can do, remarkable things happen when we surrender. When you give up being

the driver there is a bigger driver that is going to do a much better job than you.

4. Who you are in your inner world is what determines how easily and effortlessly you create in your outer world.

5. Standing in your power is being aligned with the highest parts of yourself and knowing both your humanity and your divinity.

6. You know you are standing in your power when you feel empowered—you don't want for anything.

SET SAIL WHILE THE
SAILING IS GOOD

The tapestry of life is stitched together
by a unifying knowledge manifested from joy.
—Bill Levacy

I spent twenty-five years in corporate America, the last eighteen in senior- to executive-level management in information technology. I had tremendous opportunities, made great money, and overall enjoyed myself.

This is how Lynn Carnes described her life before she took The Passion Test about a year ago. She shares the story of what has happened since getting clear on her passions.

But for most of the last ten years, a voice inside kept getting louder and louder. "I want out," it was saying. "I want to do something different. I really want to make a difference, live a totally different lifestyle, and follow my passions."

I kept pushing that voice away. I changed companies twice during that time, but this voice kept getting louder and louder.

Finally, I listened. I found I had no life (on call 24/7), I was always in one, two, or even three meetings at a time while the phone was ringing off the hook, and in the background I was doing e-mails, writing reports, running projects, dealing with walk-ins. I wasn't having fun and, to use Chris and Janet's words, I was seriously contracted.

So I quit. I had money saved up and a wonderful husband who supported me. I had no clue what I was going to do. I just knew I wanted to make a difference.

I took The Passion Test. Through that experience I really got centered on what my passions are, what I wanted to do, and started building the plan to get there. It all seemed so far off at the time, but that was only a year ago. Today my life has totally and fundamentally transformed. I am completely amazed and even stunned by the abundance that has come into my life—in every facet.

Perhaps the most surprising thing was that six months into my new adventure, my husband told me how much happier he was now that I was happy and not so stressed. I had no idea how much impact my stress had on him. He told me he felt he had gotten back the woman he married. Wow!

Then I started hearing from friends and family who told me I looked ten years younger, and I was back to the person they remembered—laughing, having fun, and fun to be with again.

My first project was putting together an Internet marketing teleseminar series, and I was amazed to discover myself attracting some of the most successful people in the online world. I soon met other incredible people who are now my business partners and friends. Together we have launched a new site (www.thepassiontest.com/bad boss) helping people make the transition it took me ten years to make.

All of my partners for three different business ventures just showed up. Right at the time I needed them. Sometimes even before I knew I needed them. I have such wonderful, talented, and giving people in my life now; I don't know where to begin thanking them. And it just keeps happening.

I wake up every day jazzed. The hours I put into my business are a joy. The people I work with are a gift. We're focused on helping as many people as we can. We recommend The Passion Test to our subscribers because we truly believe in it and know that it can be an essential part of their journey to an abundant life that they love.

I used to feel stuck and stifled in my old life, even though by most people's standards I had an amazing job, great money, and all the trappings. I now have riches beyond all compare—in the life I am now living and the gift of being able to help so many others achieve the same.

Lynne's story can be your story. It's just a matter of "Intention—Attention—No Tension."

Let's review where we are:

- You've clarified your intentions by taking The Passion Test and completing the Passion Test exercises in part 1.
- You understand the law of attraction and are now practicing finding the gift in every experience.
- You've learned the role of contraction and expansion in your life. You know how to use these signals from Nature's Guidance System to move forward easily and comfortably.
- You know that taking action is crucial in traveling the cosmic highway to the life you choose to live.
- You realize that you are not the general manager of the universe. Your job is to stay open to new possibilities and let go of your concepts of how things should work out.

Acting from the State of No Tension

Action is critical. Staying open is essential. But is there anything you can do to increase the likelihood that your action will lead to success?

The most profound secret of life is given in one of the ancient Vedic texts of India: "Established in wholeness, in the state of calmness, of inner peace, perform action."

This is the real meaning of the third step in the formula we've given you to create whatever you choose to have in your life: Intention—Attention—No Tension. Acting from the state of No Tension is the key to performing action that produces powerful results. This state of No Tension is the inner state of wholeness, of calm. When the mind is calm then inspiration is natural.

Think about it. When you are contracted isn't it often the case that your mind is also agitated? Thoughts swirl. And the more you think about it the more upset you get, don't you?

This is one of the reasons why when you feel contracted the best thing you can do is stop trying. When you feel upset, it's a signal to let go, take time to rest, relax, be easy. Remember the diagram of Nature's Guidance System? Contraction is the red light saying stop, take a break.

Living a fully conscious life means noticing when you feel expanded, when you feel contracted and responding appropriately.

The principle of No Tension is like an archer who wants to hit a target. Once he has the arrow on his bow, what does he do first? He draws the arrow back on the bow, in the exact opposite direction from the target.

Isn't it interesting that to hit the target, you must first pull back, away from the target, until the arrow is at rest, yet in a state of full potential to shoot forward? To create successful action, you must first pull back, create the state of restful alertness, inner calm, and then your action will bear fruit.

How do you do that? Getting a good night's sleep, meditation, prayer, all can help create that state of inner calm. This is why meditation twice a day and daily prayer are part of our regular routine. That state of inner calm becomes a habit.

Learning to act from that state of inner calm is the critical key to everything we've shared with you. But is there anything else you can do to increase the likelihood your actions will bear fruit?

Checking the Traffic Report
on the Cosmic Highway

When we finished the first edition of *The Passion Test*, Janet gave a copy to Bob Cranson, the man who taught her meditation over thirty-five years ago.

"Janet, it's a great book," Bob said. "And you've left out a very important piece."

"What's that?" she asked.

"Someone can be completely clear about their passions, they can do all the right things, and still sometimes everything seems to go wrong. They just hit wall after wall. Don't you think you should tell your readers how they can avoid having to go through all that disappointment?"

Okay. We weren't going to share this. After all, what we've already covered in this book is a lot to take in. But there is a body of knowledge called "Jyotish" that can help you avoid a lot of heartache and disappointment. Jyotish is a secret known to few in the Western world, and it can make a huge difference in how much you enjoy the path to living your destiny.

So we'll share this secret, and you decide what its value is for you. After all, for us, when it comes to living our passions, we use every tool that may be helpful. We would expect nothing less for you.

First Janet will give you her experience of the power of Jyotish and the effect it had on a very important moment in her life.

When Chris and I were married, we used to visit a Jyotishi (an expert is this area) and have an annual Jyotish reading to see what trends or predictions they might have for us.

We had always been taught that Jyotish is for the purpose of "averting the danger before it occurs." When you know the future tendencies, you can adjust your actions appropriately to achieve the best results. We wanted to make sure we had a clear understanding of anything in our lives that could be a challenge or an opportunity, so we could adjust accordingly.

After Chris had finished getting his reading with an Indian Jyotishi and his translator, there were still ten minutes left. Being one to seize the moment, I asked the Jyotishi if I could use Chris's remaining ten minutes for my questions.

"Yes" was the reply.

"Can you tell me anything about my mother?" I asked.

The Jyotishi started making calculations, and after some minutes he turned to me with a very somber tone and said, "You must go see your mother immediately. We can't tell you she is going to die, but you must go see her immediately."

Chills went through my spine. My mother was in the hospital in Los Angeles, California, and there was no way the Jyotishi could have known this.

"Are you 100 percent sure?" I asked.

"Yes," he replied.

"And when you go see her," he said, "take gifts and flowers and tell her all the things you love about her. Say all the things you want her forgiveness for, make your amends."

Even though it would stretch our finances to the limit, Chris and I decided we had to do what the Jyotishi said. His advice in the past had been pretty accurate, and if there was a chance my mom might pass away soon, I didn't want to take the chance of not healing my relationship with her.

My mother had been my best friend until I was seven and then she became an alcoholic. When that happened my world changed completely. My parents broke up because of her drinking, and she ended up either in alcoholic homes or in depressing motels. For the last six years she had finally stopped drinking and become a Seventh-Day Adventist.

I had a lot of pent-up emotions surrounding my relationship with my mother and the times when she was drinking. I had never discussed these with her, and it was time to let them go. I especially felt badly about the anger I had shown toward her and the way I had treated her during some of her most challenging times. I knew if there was a possibility of her passing away, I had a deep desire to complete some things with her beforehand.

The next day I drove to Iowa City and bought my mother lots of beautiful presents. Three days later, Chris and I were on our way to L.A.

"Momper Stompers" (the name I had given her when I was little) was sitting on her bed smiling from ear to ear, looking like the picture of health when we walked in.

I was happy that she looked so great but totally perturbed at myself for listening to the Jyotishis and their predictions. It was obvious from the rosy glow of Mom's cheeks that they were way off.

I gave Mompers the presents I brought her and decided to make the best use of this time, whatever the future held. I spent hours and hours sharing all of the things I had always wanted to say to her and never did.

"Mompers," I said, my voice cracking with emotion as I began. "I am so sorry I wasn't there for you when you needed me the most. I was so angry with you and I felt so abandoned when you started drinking . . ."

As I shared with my mom, tears started streaming down both of our faces.

I went on. "Mompers, you're the reason I love people so much. Did I ever tell you that? It's true. My friends even get mad at me because they say it's not right for me to tell everyone I love them. They say it's not possible to love everybody. But I do, Mompers. I really do, and it's all because of the love you showered on me when I was so little. I never forgot that love. And it was your love. You did that for me. You gave me the greatest gift of all."

"Oh, Jani," my Mompers said with tears in her eyes. "I wasn't a failure to you?" she cried, breaking into uncontrollable sobs.

"Oh no, Mompers, you are my heart! You taught me what it really means to love."

"You were always my little angel," she said.

As she said those words we both sat there in the hospital holding each other, washing away years of pain as we cried in each other's arms.

After three emotionally rich days with my mom, Chris and I flew back to Iowa. Two days after our return my mother called me.

"Guess what?" she said happily.

"What, Mompers?" I asked.

"The doctors said I am doing so well I get to go home."

"Wow, that's great news!"

While I was so happy to hear about my mom's clean bill of health, I was furious at the Jyotishi for his obviously wrong prediction. The trip to California had been a lot for us financially, and I would much have preferred to make the trip later when things were a little easier.

Immediately after hanging up with my mother I faxed a scathing note to the Jyotishi telling him I was shocked that they would make a mistake about something so important.

A few hours later a fax from the Jyotishi came back with his short reply.

"It is always good to visit your mother."

Now I was really steaming. Did they think this was a joke? I was beyond irritated.

A few days later, my sister, Mickey, called me. "Janet, get on a plane. Mom's dying." It seems Mom had an unexpected, severe relapse and had refused life support.

I got on the next plane available and as I was in the air, I knew exactly when Mom died. I was meditating and all of a sudden, I just knew she was gone.

When I got to L.A., I rented a car and drove to the hospital, praying that my premonition on the plane was wrong. I wanted so much to spend those last moments with my mom.

Knees wobbling, I walked up to the front desk and asked the day nurse if I could see Dena Miller, all the while holding my breath in painful anticipation of what her words would say.

"Oh, I'm sorry dear, Dena Miller died this morning," she said matter-of-factly.

When she saw the shocked look on my face, she blurted, "Oh my God, are you family? I thought all of the family had been here this morning. Oh honey, I am so sorry. Let me take you to this little room where you can be with yourself. You can stay there as long as you need. Do you want any water? Is there anything I can get you?"

"No, I'm okay. I just need to be alone."

Once in the little room the tears started to fall. I wasn't crying more than three minutes when all of a sudden my mood totally shifted and a smile appeared on my face. I felt such a sense of completion and connection with my mom—all I could feel was love and joy.

"No, you can't do that!" I said to myself. "Your mother just died."

And there it was again, this huge smile, now followed by waves of happiness.

"Will you stop that and cry!" I said to myself. "This is your mother, and she just died. What's wrong with you? It's not right to be happy. How can you be so unfeeling?"

And still, no matter how hard I tried, this silly grin just kept showing up followed by waves and waves of deep inner happiness.

Finally, realizing that my feelings were out of my control, I surrendered to the incredibly blissful feeling that had overtaken me (at the most inappropriate time) and walked out of the hospital with a smile on my face as big as the universe.

"Mother is here and she is happy," was my next thought. "Oh my God . . . Mother is here . . . and she really is happy!"

Singing at the top of my lungs and feeling so full inside, I drove my rental car at top speed to my mother's apartment, hoping I would find my sister Mickey still there. I wanted so much to share the good news that I knew that Mother is now *really* happy, after spending a lifetime in suffering and struggle.

I sensed a presence with me in the car.

"You were complete," the voice said as I was driving. "You made your amends."

I immediately saw the word *amends* inside my head and realized it means "*to mend.*"

"You were complete," the words again spoke from inside of me. "You mended everything. The Jyotishis told you what you needed to do and you did it. You said your amends so there is nothing for you to regret."

"Another meaning for amends," the voice continued, "is '*amen.*'"

This experience changed my life in profound ways. It taught me the power of timing and the value of Jyotish. Not that Jyotish is always 100 percent accurate, but it is a profound tool to help in creating the life you choose to live.

We share this story to give you a sense of the remarkable outcomes that are possible from knowing the tendencies of things to come. It would not be useful to base your entire life on Jyotish predictions. At the same time, they can be a valuable additional input to the decisions you have to make.

As applied to living your passions, here's the basic principle: you can increase the likelihood of success by being alert to the timing of when you choose to take action.

We can hear you now, "What's the big secret about that? Everyone knows that timing can make all the difference." In fact, haven't we all heard the saying, "Timing is everything"?

What most people don't know, or have only heard misleading rumors about, is that there is a discipline for predicting tendencies or probabilities of future outcomes based on when any significant action is begun. You can use this discipline to plan the timing of your projects to have the greatest likelihood of achieving successful results. You can also use it to take action to avoid undesirable consequences, just as Janet did.

Think about it this way: if you're getting on the cosmic highway with a new project, you can get on when the traffic is backed up and it will take forever to get where you want to go, or you can time your trip to begin when the road is clear and you can go ahead at full speed.

We are all used to checking the traffic reports before we begin a journey. And we've grown accustomed to listening to the weather report before setting out on a long trip. Even though the weatherman may not always be right, most of us have found listening to the predictions of meteorologists valuable.

In a similar manner, Jyotish is an ancient discipline for determining when conditions are favorable to begin any major new activity in your life. Jyotish is traditionally defined as "the science of time determination."

For those of you who are skeptics, here is an opportunity for you to practice staying open. Who knows? You just might be surprised.

Have you figured out yet that everything in our world is connected with everything else? While analyzing differences can be of value in understanding how the parts fit together, you will find your life and your work most rewarding when you give attention to the connections between people and things in your world, rather than the differences. This includes the connections between the physical world and the activities you intend to undertake.

Have you noticed that Nature moves in cycles? Night and day. Winter, spring, summer, and fall. High tide and low tide. These cycles are a function of the movement of our planet and its movement relative to the moon and the sun. These cycles have a big impact on our experience of life.

Jyotish is the study of these cycles, based on the movements of the earth on its axis, its movement around the sun, and the rotation of our solar system around the center of our galaxy. It dates back beyond recorded history. It is a combination of understanding the cycles of Nature and the correlations of those cycles with human activity, observed over a very long period of time.

Jyotish does not tell you what is going to happen in your life. It provides predictions of future tendencies or probabilities. Nothing is set in stone. But with this knowledge you can time the launching of new projects or the best time for beginning new endeavors so the likelihood of success is greatest.

When you understand that we live in an interconnected universe in which every part affects every other part, there is a world of possibility to explore that most people have never dreamt of. We invite you to begin exploring.

Making use of Jyotish can be as simple as finding a qualified Jyotishi and requesting a reading. You can expect to pay a fee. Usually this is a couple of hundred dollars for an hour review of the tendencies in your life from a qualified person. If you don't want to pay the money, Bill Levacy has written some great books on the subject, which can get you started.

The first session with a Jyotishi is generally a review of your entire life. They will tell you many things you probably already know, and they will tell you the tendencies of your life to come. Included in this session can be valuable information about the sorts of activities in which you are most likely to experience success.

After this first session, you can choose to have an annual review, called a "progression," to go over the tendencies for the coming year to give you an idea of what to expect and when it is best to begin various activities. One of the services we make most use of is the determination of a *muhurta* or "auspicious time."

For significant events in your life, such as a marriage, moving into a new home, signing a contract, or starting a new venture, beginning on a date and time that is auspicious can make all the difference between an easy, comfortable experience and one that is full of struggle and challenge. This is the equivalent of "setting sail while the sailing is good."

In addition to Bill Levacy, our friend Christina Collins Hill is a world-class Jyotish expert whom we have known for years, consult frequently, and strongly recommend. See the resources section at the back of the book for more information.

When you stay open, you may discover that all sorts of interesting possibilities appear in your life. Our suggestion is to be open, to listen, to test out new possibilities for yourself, and then use those tools and that knowledge which resonate with your own experience of life. You'll begin to discover that even if staying open is a bit uncomfortable at first, it can be a heck of a lot of fun as you get the hang of it.

Timing is everything, and plenty of people have hit the timing perfectly, even without Jyotish. Richard Paul Evans wrote a story for his two children that ended up becoming a multimillion-copy bestseller. We found his story to be an incredible inspiration for us, and we think you will too. As you read the following interview, notice that when you are truly aligned with your passions, failure is not an option.

Richard Paul Evans

When Richard Paul Evans wrote the #1 New York Times *bestseller* The Christmas Box, *he never intended to become an internationally known author. Officially, he was an advertising executive, an award-winning clay animator for the American and Japanese markets, a candidate for state legislature, and, most importantly, a husband and father.*

His quiet story of parental love and the true meaning of Christmas made history when his self-published book became simultaneously the number one hardcover and paperback book in the nation. Since then, more than 8 million copies of The Christmas Box *have been printed.*

His latest book is called The Five Lessons a Millionaire Taught Me.

"When I first wrote *The Christmas Box*, I felt this tremendous love for my children, and it was something brand new in a way. I didn't necessarily want to have children, and when I made that decision, I didn't know how it would affect my life. It opened up so many doors and changed my life in so many ways that when I wrote *The Christmas Box* I wanted to somehow capture that. I wanted to share with people the joy that comes from the service of raising children.

"*The Christmas Box* wasn't a book that was to be published or spread around the world. I wanted to capture that feeling so that someday when my children held their own children in their arms, they could think of and understand how I felt about them, as a father.

"Initially, my whole idea was to make two copies of the book, one for each of my children. When I finished the book, I was so moved by the experience that I wanted to share it with people, so I gave a copy to my wife, Keri, and she was moved by it as well.

"I started to share it with family and friends and decided that rather than making two copies I was going to make twenty copies. We were going to make them Christmas presents, so that's what we did. I went out, made twenty copies, and handed them out as Christmas presents, and that's where it all started.

"I started receiving phone calls almost every single day from people reading the book. About six weeks after I gave those books out as Christmas presents, I received a phone call from a local bookstore.

"The clerk just said, 'Hello, Mr. Evans. Did you write a Christmas story?' I said, yes. She said, 'Oh good. Where can we order it?'

"'You can't order it. The book's never been published,' I answered. She said, 'Well, I've had ten orders for that book this week.'

"The first thing to remember about this story is that it was *the book*. It took on a life of its own. The book was special. Even though I've become a savvier marketer, I have not been able to duplicate the success of *The Christmas Box* since.

"When I started, the first thing I realized was that because I was passionate about it, I actually had an advantage being self-published. When you work with a larger publisher, it's a business. They're good at what they do, but they're going to put out more than a hundred different books. So they throw a book out there. If it doesn't work right off, then they'll probably drop it.

"As a self-published book, I cared a lot about it. I was willing to go to bat for the book. I believed in the destiny of the book. I had a belief that if people just read it they would change, and that's what I found.

"I remember the first time I met Jack Canfield and Mark Victor Hansen. I was at my very first book show. *Chicken Soup for the Soul* was just taking off. My idea was, 'I'm going to go there and give away five thousand copies of my book because I believe that if five thousand people read my book they will take it out and spread it, and it will become a number one bestseller.'

"I started to practice what I call guerrilla marketing. I know there's now a book about that, but I was calling it that before the book. It's like, 'Okay, if I can't win the big war against the big publishers, how *can* I win?' Well, I can be, if not a big fish, at least a medium-sized fish in a small pond. I can win in the little markets.

"I would go to little cities no one cared about and get on the radio. They were looking for something to talk about. I could tell them about my book, and I began to learn what people were connecting with in the book. I learned why they liked the book and what affected them and why they wanted to share it. As I learned those things, I got to the point where I would go on these radio interviews and my distributor could actually track me around the country because every time I would give a radio interview they would get four or five calls from bookstores in that city, looking for the book.

"I don't know if you've studied the life of Ronald Reagan at all, but in the early days he signed a contract with, I believe it was General Motors. He hated to speak, and he wasn't very good at it. People would walk out on him. Because he did so much speaking, he decided, 'I'm going to get good at this.' He started to work very hard at getting good at it, and he came to be known, throughout history, as 'the great communicator.'

"My first interviews for *The Christmas Box* weren't very good. They weren't interviews on radio—I was talking to people at book signings. People would come up and say, 'What is this?' At first, if I'd tell people, they'd walk away. They weren't that interested. Then one day I came across something that made them say, 'Oh, that sounds interesting. I'll buy the book.' I was learning, and so I would find another thing.

"What I learned near the end was, more than half the time, if someone talked to me, they would buy the book. So I learned what sold the book. I learned how to speak about it, and I was able to talk from a level of passion. If I didn't care about the book, it never would have happened, but they saw that passion coming through me, and they wanted to share it, so they would buy the book. Then, after they bought the book, they would read it and they'd come back to buy more, because they wanted to share the message.

"I think anytime you're following your passions you're going to be tested. There are things that test how much we really care about something.

"I was at the Mountains and Plains book show in Colorado. I didn't have a lot of money. I took all the money I had and put it toward marketing. I went to this book show and I'm there, handing out copies of my book, meeting bookstore owners.

"But no one was coming through the main area where the booths were. I was frustrated, so finally I went up and asked someone who was walking through, 'Where is everyone? There are thousands of people here. How come there's no one in the hall?' He said, 'Well, because they're out with the authors.'

"I walked out, and sure enough the publishers would bring in some of the top authors in America and give away free books, so these bookstore owners would stand in line and get all these books for free, autographed. Then they'd go, get back in line, and wait for the next slug of authors to come through.

"So I'm sitting out there watching this happen and watching my dreams vanish, because I'm a nobody. No one cares I'm at the show. No one knows who I am, and here are famous authors. So I'm sitting there watching.

"All of a sudden, I had this thought. I looked up at the table and there was an empty seat. I thought, 'What is stopping me, besides security and the people at the show, from just walking up there and sitting with the authors?' I looked at the tables, and I'm shy. I thought, there is no way. I turned around and started to walk away.

Then it just hit me. 'How much do you care about this book?' That was one of those gut honest moments when it's like, 'Well, I care a lot.'

"Then, 'If you don't do it, who will?' I bit my tongue, I turned around, and walked up around the back. I came through the curtain and sat down between two bestselling authors. I was absolutely terrified. Then the worst thing that could happen . . . one of the organizers, of course, immediately spotted me.

"The woman walks over to me, and right when she gets to me, I looked up and said, 'Sorry I'm late.' The woman was stunned. She looked at me for a moment, blinked, and she said, 'May I get you some water?' I said, 'Sure.'

"I sat there and finished out this whole long line of people coming through, sitting next to bestselling authors, signing my books. The next year, I came back as the number one bestselling author in the country. I was the featured author at the entire show. People were in line to see me.

"That same woman was there the next year. I walked up and said, 'Do you remember me, per chance?' She smiled and said, 'Yes, I do. Good for you.' I said, 'Thank you for not throwing me out.' She said, 'Honestly, I was going to. That's my job. I was walking over to tell you to leave. When you looked up and I saw the earnestness in your eyes, I thought, what is it going to hurt? Now here is someone chasing his dream, as crazy as he may be. It's not going to hurt anyone to let him sit here and give away his book.' So she got me water instead of throwing me out, and look how it came back to bless both of us.

"That, to me, was one of those gut-check moments when I asked, do I really have passion? When people say, "You're so lucky," it's like, no, you have no idea. I was willing to fight for this book. I was willing to do uncomfortable things. I was willing to take chances. I was willing to risk everything for this book. Failure simply was not an option.

"When you have that kind of passion, fate favors the bold. All of a sudden things will just start. You will struggle and you'll fight, but you will win.

"If you remember nothing else from our discussion here, remember this. We do not succeed in spite of our obstacles and challenges. We succeed precisely because of them. I want to repeat that. *We do not succeed in spite of our obstacles and challenges. We succeed precisely because of them.*

"Fear is the opposite of faith. Fear is something you recognize for what it is. You can't have fear and faith at the same time in your mind, because faith is simply a state of mind. Fear can help you recognize reality and that's a service and that's a good thing. But when you're ready to move, then you don't take counsel from fear, you let it go. It's like, okay, I'm going to overcome that. I believe I can do this.

"Whatever you want to accomplish, having a sense of destiny is the starting point. I had a complete sense of destiny with *The Christmas Box*. If you have that sense of destiny, it will lead you where you need to go. That is the underlying tone of everything we talked about. Without it, if you don't believe there's a destiny or divinity to our lives, then it's all a crap shoot anyway."

What were the key lessons from this interview about living your passion?

1. Unexpected support begins to show up when you're aligned with what you're supposed to be doing, doors open in ways you couldn't have predicted.

2. Sometimes there's an advantage to doing it yourself, when you're passionate about it. For example, Richard's self-published book may have been more successful than if it had gone through a major publisher.

3. When you're passionate, you may not be good at what you're doing in the beginning. But if you have to do it to follow your passions, experience will make you good at it.

4. Passion can be contagious. When people hear your passion, they want to be part of it.

5. Anytime you're following your passions, you're going to be tested. Things will show up to test how much you care about something.

6. When you're passionate, you will be willing to fight for your passions, to do uncomfortable things, to take chances, to risk everything.

7. We do not succeed in spite of our obstacles and challenges. We succeed precisely because of them.

8. Success comes from making mistakes and learning from them.

9. Fear is the opposite of faith. You can't have fear and faith at the same time. When you're ready to move, you let go of the fear.

10. When you're passionate, failure is not an option.

11. When you have a sense of destiny, it will lead you where you need to go.

IT'S ABOUT
EVERYONE ELSE

The key of all life is value.
Value is not what you get,
it's what you give.
—*Jay Abraham*

My name is Lorena Espinosa. I am thirty-three years old. I am from Mexico. I have two daughters and am married to a man I met on the Internet. He came to meet me and five months after we met I married him. I know . . . too fast! I did not know how hard it was going to be for me to get used to living in a new country, with a different language, missing my family, and starting a new life as a wife.

My husband is nineteen years older than me and sometimes he has a strong temper. I didn't know how to deal with his temper. I felt totally alone and bad. I suffered a lot from depression . . . one day even trying to commit suicide. I was taking Prozac and there are a lot of things that have not been okay in my life.

Then I discovered The Passion Test. Your book touched me so much!

I have been trying to change my life. I created my list of top passions.

When my life is ideal:

1. My job is productive and successful helping others to have a better life. I am touching their lives.
2. I have control of my own life, am able to support myself and take care of my two daughters and my family in Mexico.
3. I live in accordance with my values in a happy environment.

Now it's nine months later and things have gotten much better. The Passion Test helped me rediscover what I really love and want for my life.

I still have some issues I have not been able to address the way I would like . . . but things have improved so much. For example, it's been a long time since I have had another big depression.

When I took The Passion Test for the first time, I was working at an office supply store for $7.50 an hour. I realized the pay was too low, so I took a job for the holidays at a department store, which paid $8.50 an hour. But I was still not doing my ideal work.

I really like people and helping them grow. I have been an Avon representative for seven years, but I hadn't done much with it.

When I found myself without a job, and began thinking about my passions, I realized that my Avon business would allow me to do things I love the most. So three and a half months ago I started working at my Avon business like I never have before.

I've begun leading meetings where I give motivational training and do what I love to do: be in front of people, helping them transform their lives. I combine showing them the advantage of the Avon business with the importance of growing as a person.

I had a meeting a month ago and there were so many people that my next meeting will be in a hotel. In just this short time my business has grown from twenty-five people to eighty-one, and counting. Most of my people are Hispanics. I have moved up to the next level in leadership so now I am making a good income ... doing what I love and being able to be at home with my girls.

The Passion Test opened my eyes and gave me the open door to pursue what I really love to do. Somehow like "magic" everything started to work for me. Even my husband has started to control his temper. We still need to work a lot on our relationship, but now it is so much easier because I see that I will be able to do what I love.

Janet and Chris's book is always with me on my desk ... to remind me that I need to do what I love to be happy.

A few months later we got another note from Lorena, just before this went to our publisher. Here's her latest update:

Let me tell you my life is good and I just cannot believe how good I feel!

Every day I wake up and repeat in my mind how my perfect life will be—and it is happening.

A week ago my husband gave me a thousand dollars and helped choose a car for me. He has never done something like this before. I will pay for the rest of the cost of my car, but it is mine. I can go wherever I want. This is a miracle! I used to need him to drive me wherever I needed to go and couldn't go anywhere unless he was available to drive me. Now I am in control of where I go.

My Avon team is growing like crazy. I now have over 150 people in my organization and every day I put more people in my downline. I've reached executive unit leader and I am planning to grow more and more.

When I was working in retail stores the pay was by the hour. Now my earnings are based on my performance, and I am making much more than I ever did working by the hour. I am not rich . . . yet! But I am doing what I love. I love to be around people and to help them.

The book was the beginning for me to start living happily, doing what I love to do.

Lorena's story illustrates two very important principles about living your passions. First, when you begin choosing in favor of your passions your life will begin to transform in ways you can't predict. Second, aligning your life with your passions is a

process. There are still challenges to face. Yet when you are living your passions and giving attention to the good in your life,
those challenges are so much easier to deal with.

The key is to get out of your own way. There are only three
things (which are really one thing) that can prevent you from
living a passionate life. They are:

- False ideas
- False concepts
- False beliefs

False ideas, concepts, and beliefs are things you've come to believe are true that simply don't match reality, even though you
may think they do. Thinking "I am worthless" or "I can't do it"
or "I'm not good enough" are examples of the kinds of false
beliefs that can keep you from getting on the cosmic highway
to fulfilling your purpose in life.

Some Driving Tips on the Cosmic Highway

Earlier we told you that "What you love and God's will for you
are one and the same." Some people might think, "How can it
be true that an alcoholic's love for alcohol, a drug addict's love
for drugs, or a libertine's love for sex, are God's will for
them?"

While people may say an alcoholic "loves" alcohol, this is a
different meaning of love from when we say what you love,
your passions, are the things you care most deeply about in
your life.

Janet knows from personal experience:

When I was little, my mom and I were inseparable. She called me her "little angel" and we had such a deep bond. She took me everywhere and when it came time for me to go to kindergarten, we both cried our eyes out at the thought that we wouldn't be able to spend our days together.

In fact, from time to time it was too much for my mother. She would make some excuse and take me out of school, just so we could be together. I so loved those days. It was the happiest time of my life.

When I was seven years old everything changed. Mom began working as a hairstylist and coming home drunk. She and my dad would get into huge arguments. No walls could contain the words they exchanged, and my little heart was broken.

The sweet, beautiful voice that used to sing me to sleep at night was gone. The precious days of being by my mother's side were history. In their place was a drunken, unhappy woman who had to be undressed and put to bed at night.

After weeks and months of urging and begging and demanding that she stop drinking, my father finally piled me, my sister, and brother into the car and left, with my mother running after us, asking for one more chance. I can't even begin to describe the heartbreak I felt.

As the years went by, my mother sank deep into her self-inflicted hell. I remember searching through the flea-bitten motels on Main Street in Los Angeles, only to find her half-unconscious in a drunken stupor. Eventually, she became a Seventh-Day Adventist, turned the tide on her drinking, and lived out a quiet, modest life.

When I look back now, as an adult, I see that my

> mom's drinking was her attempt to dull the pain of feeling she was worthless and unworthy. Her father had molested her when she was a little girl, then kidnapped her when he left her mother. Mom had deep fears of abandonment from her childhood experiences. From a child's perspective, why would she be abandoned? Because she is not lovable. Drinking was her desperate attempt to make the pain stop.

The alcoholic, the drug addict, and the libertine lust rather than love. They lust after what they believe will make them feel better. (See what we mean about "false beliefs"?) Passion and lust are two very different things.

Lust arises from a sense of lack. It is driven by an overpowering need to fill something that is missing inside or to dull a pain too great to feel. When we lust after something, we are trying to fill a void. Janet's mother felt worthless and inadequate. Those feelings were way too painful to feel, so she tried to make the pain stop by drinking.

These feelings of pain are Nature's Guidance System, trying to tell us to stop, make a change, take care of ourselves, nurture ourselves. But when you ignore the signal and instead try to make it stop by dulling the pain through alcohol or drugs or sex or food or whatever, you keep moving down the line toward increasing misery and suffering.

Your passions, on the other hand, are the most significant loves in your life. They arise from deep within the heart. Passion will draw you irresistibly along the path of your destiny. It connects you with the most profound part of your own nature. When you are aligned with your passions, you will feel expanded, open, turned on. Passion takes us up the line toward increasing joy and fulfillment.

This is why Nature's Guidance System is so important. The pursuit of lust may lead to temporary happiness, but very quickly this fleeting happiness becomes an awful contraction. Ignore that contraction, dull yourself to the pain of feeling it, and you will find yourself moving faster and faster down toward misery and suffering.

The decision to enter rehab or counseling or some other means to change one's behavior in a more life-supporting direction brings a wave of hope, of expansion. That is the signal to move forward, take action.

When you have clearly identified your top five passions, and you understand the nature of contraction and expansion, the pursuit of your destiny or purpose in life truly becomes effortless. You just need to remember:

**Whenever you are faced
with a choice, a decision, or an opportunity,
choose in favor of your passions.**

This means, ask yourself, "Will making this decision help me become more aligned with my passions, or will it move me farther away?" If it will help you become more aligned then make that decision. If it will move you farther away from living your passions then learn to say, "No, and thank you for asking."

Once having made the decision, pay attention to the cosmic guidance system. Notice when you feel contracted and take a break. Rest, come back to yourself, and take it easy.

When you feel expanded, move forward, take action, and enjoy the fulfillment that comes.

There are some in this world who have been very successful in driving along the cosmic highway. They have achieved a level of fulfillment that leads others to seek them out as role models.

Pujya Swamiji Chidanand Saraswati is one such individual. He is revered by millions throughout India. He is the spiritual inspiration of Parmarth Niketan, an ashram on the banks of the Ganges River in Rishikesh, India. You will discover in his words some universal truths that apply to all of us, whatever our religion or spiritual direction:

There is no magic wand we can wave and create a perfect life for ourselves. Life itself is magic. Dedicate yourselves to living what you want the future to manifest. If you want to receive love, very simple, give love. And if you want to have friends, become a good friend. If you want a connection with God, reach out to him. He is waiting for us.

What we must realize is, "I am part of God's creation. As He is perfect, so I am perfect. As He is divine, so I am divine. As He wills, so it will unfold in the right way."

You are part and parcel of the divine. He is divine. You are divine. He is perfect. You are perfect. Of course, we are all different. We all have different strengths and weaknesses, but each of us is perfect in our own way. Each of us has our own role to fulfill on this earth.

Serving humanity is the greatest, truest joy in the world. I have seen this, not only in my life, but in thousands of people's lives.

When someone gives something to us, we are momentarily happy. We become happy, but that happiness is not there all the time.

When we give something, we become eternally happy. You can see this, even in children. When they get a new toy, they are so happy for a very short while. But when you take a child to see poor or sick children, you will see the deep joy and satisfaction the child gets out of sharing.

The reason for this is that it is part of the divine plan. We are put here on earth to serve.

Helping Others Is Helping Yourself

It is a fascinating paradox that the way to have everything you want in your life is to help others have everything they want in their lives. Those who are spiritual, like Pujya Swamiji, interpret this principle in spiritual terms, but you don't have to be spiritual to discover the truth of it.

The same principle applies in business. The success of your business is based on the value you provide to your customers. Providing value is, by definition, helping others have what they consider valuable.

Our friend and colleague Jay Abraham would tell you he is not a particularly spiritual man. Yet he has lived by this principle throughout his career. As a result, he has made millions of dollars, owns beautiful homes, is flown first class all over the world, and has achieved a level of success and recognition most people would find enviable.

Here's how Jay talks about his passions and the importance of helping others to help yourself.

Jay Abraham

Jay Abraham has worked with over ten thousand small and medium-sized businesses, adding billions of dollars in revenues to their income statements. It's no surprise that Forbes magazine listed him as one of the five top executive coaches in the world, saying Jay's specialty is "Turning corporate underperformers into marketing and sales whizzes."

Jay has been acknowledged as a unique and distinctive authority in the field of business performance enhancement—and the maximizing and multiplying of business assets. He's spawned an entire generation of marketing consultants and experts who credit him as their primary mentor. Nearly two thousand websites reference his successful work on the Internet alone.

He is the author of Getting Everything You Can Out of All You've Got. *Here's what Jay has to say about his own passions and about what it takes to create the life you choose to live.*

"For those of you who haven't achieved all your goals yet, irrespective of your age, one of the most wonderful realities is that material goals, when and if you achieve them, are not, by themselves, going to transform your life.

"It's certainly nice to have enough economic security to be able to live where you want and eat what you want and have some of the trappings you want, but once you get the 'stuff' you want, you realize there's a lot more to life than just things, status, and stature.

"I've done a lot. I've had a lot. I've experienced a lot. But I've also really subordinated factors in my life as I've gotten older, as my health has become more of a concern to me, as I've watched children grow and loved ones die, and seen the ones most important to me not be as close as I would have liked—I've slowed down and recalibrated what's relevant.

"Today one of my top passions is having balance in my life. I used to be a workaholic and monstrously committed. I'd work eighteen hours a day, seven days a week, and have meetings at two in the morning. Now, though, if my wife calls and says, 'Let's go to lunch,' unless I have a very, very important meeting, I'll stop and do that, because in the scope of forever, that's more important. I want balance—economic, intellectual, spiritual, physical, sexual—all kinds of balanced stimulation at a level that's very healthy.

"If you can't be passionate about something or someone, you shouldn't even have that in your life because you're stealing the experience from them and from you. Why be half-invested in anything? Why do anything and accept half of the outcome, half the result, half of the payoff? There is a great payoff from being passionate. Passionate is probably the most selfish thing you can be because you get so much more out of it.

"Being passionate has great positive benefits, and ignoring your passions brings a great cost. In the positive, my passion for wanting to see a business owner be so much more than they are; my passion for knowing how much more was possible from the day, from the investment, from the opportunity, from an advertisement, from a competitive environment; my passion for having a vision for somebody that was greater than they even had for themselves because I knew what they could do; my passion for having enough faith in a client or a business because I knew how much more they could contribute to their community and their marketplace and their prospective client—these things are what drove billions and billions of dollars to be created, because I believed in my clients and ultimately they believed more deeply in themselves.

"In my personal life I haven't been as focused on my passions. I put too much of my time in my business, and I've lost relationships. I can say it goes both ways. Lack of passion costs you dearly, and sometimes you don't know the cost because it's a compound bill. When it comes due it is very painful.

"Passion needs to be balanced, and passion needs to be universal in your life. If you can't be passionate, if you can't really fall in love with what you're doing, who you're doing it for or with, and the result of it, shame on you. Do it full out.

"If I were you, each and every one of you reading this, I would take Chris and Janet's Passion Test. Then tomorrow morning, start looking at the people you interact with in your life. If you have a wife or a husband or a significant other, if you have children, family members, that you are frustrated with, tired of, don't get what you think you want from them, feel choked or claustrophobic about—start looking at what's great about them.

"Find something that's really neat about them. Find the one thing about them that's really cool, really interesting, really impressive, really amazing, really wonderful, really remarkable, and keep doing that every day. Think of the thing about them that you love among everything else. Think about what is the most impressive thing about them. Think about their greatest attribute, whether you admire it or not, whether it's their work ethic or their discipline or their joy of living or whatever it is, and start appreciating and understanding them.

"It's your job in life to observe, examine, appreciate, understand, and respect how many different ways everyone else sees the same thing you're going through. Maybe you don't agree 100 percent, but if you appreciate it, if you respect it, if you examine it, if you observe it objectively and without prejudgment, it just makes life so much more dimensional, fascinating, fun, educational, and informative.

"The key of all life is value. Value is not what you get, it's what you give. It's figuring out what's important to other people, not just to you. I had to ask myself, how do I think I'm going to have an extraordinary, fluid relationship with my wife and children?

"Do you think it will work if I yell, 'Hey you guys, I want to be connected'? Do you think that's going to do it? Or am I going to have a higher probability of success by first figuring out what's important to them, what they like, what they enjoy, what rings their bell, what rocks their boat, what brings them happiness—and trying to connect with them on that level, first and foremost?

"I mean, it's real simple. It's very elegant in its purity. Think about what's important to them, whoever "they" are, whether it's business, whether it's your employer. If you work for somebody else, figure out what problems they're struggling with, figure out what's going to make them more secure, what's going to make them more successful.

"With somebody above you, figure out what's going to get them a raise, what's going to get them a promotion, what's going to get them acknowledgment, and that will get you what you want.

"We're so consumed with us, us, us. The real fast-track path to getting everything, anything, and more than everything you want is putting others ahead of what you want and focusing on their needs, their wants, their desires, and fulfilling them.

"It's not manipulative, it's great joy. It's greatly fulfilling to help others grow, develop, gain fulfillment and enrichment.

"You will find that in order to be successful you have to first want to make other people successful. In order to be loved you have to first love; in order to be interesting you have to first be interested. The mere opposite of what you want is what you have to give first and then you will get back the desired result or outcome in droves.

"Most people ask the wrong questions. The right question is not, 'Am I worthy of the goal,' but, 'Is the goal worthy of me?' When you realize how much more you can do, how much more you can impact, how much more you can contribute, how much more you can achieve, how much more you can enrich people at all levels—tangibly, intangibly, spiritually, emotionally, physically—by your body of work, by being on this planet, by interacting, then you are going to raise the bar. You're going to knock out all the false ceilings. My goal is to do that for a lot of people.

"The biggest reason most people don't achieve the enrichment they want on both financial and emotional levels is their self-focus. It isn't about you, it's about everyone else, and when you make everyone else's life better, your life automatically opens up and expands monstrously.

"It's about falling in love with other people, what you're doing for them, and getting clear on what your life is all about.

"It's audacious and ludicrous to flagellate yourself for what you haven't achieved if you don't first go through this very clarifying, expedient, and absolutely immutable and unerring process that will get you whatever it is you want faster, easier; and you won't just achieve it, you will easily and profoundly exceed whatever you set for yourself if you turn your attention to what you can give to others."

What were the key lessons from this interview about living your passion?

1. Material goals, by themselves, are not going to transform your life.

2. Why be half-invested in anything? There is a great payoff from being passionate.

3. Lack of passion costs you dearly, and sometimes you don't know the cost because it's a compound bill that can be very painful when it comes due.

4. Find the one thing in those you interact with in your life that is really cool, really interesting, really impressive, really remarkable and use these things to start appreciating and understanding those closest to you.

5. The key of all life is value. Value is not what you get, it's what you give. It's figuring out what's important to other people, not just you.

6. The real fast track to getting everything, anything, and more than everything you want is putting others ahead of what you want and focusing on their needs, their wants, their desires, and fulfilling them.

7. In order to be successful, you have to first want to make others successful. To be loved, you have to first love. To be interesting, you have to first be interested.

8. To find your passions and create balance, stretch—ask a lot of questions and examine a lot of different realities.

9. The right question is not, "Am I worthy of the goal," but, "Is the goal worthy of me?"

10. The biggest reason most people don't achieve enrichment on both financial and emotional levels is their self-focus. It isn't about you, it's about everyone else, and when you make everyone else's life better, your life automatically opens up.

TRAVELING AT THE SPEED OF TRUST

Trust is a great form of motivation—
of releasing talent, energy, passion—
of releasing your own energy and passion
by being trusted and also by extending trust to other people.

—*Stephen M. R. Covey*

My name is Otto. I'm seventy-five years old. I have type 2 diabetes and coronary artery disease. In the past I taught English in a medical school in China for a year and a half, and I absolutely loved it. I was able to make a significant difference in my students' lives, and I had a dream of going back to China to teach again.

Before discovering The Passion Test I had spent a year and a half applying to teach oral English in China, with no success. The Chinese respect and honor their elders, but they don't think they should be working. I found myself buying into those beliefs, and most of my friends told me I was too old to think about going overseas to teach again.

I had received more than twenty refusals from schools in China when I took The Passion Test and listed as one of my top five passions, "When my life is ideal I have a job in China in a desirable location."

Within a week I received an e-mail from a school in Guilin, China, saying that if I was still interested in a job to call a number and speak to Kimberley. I called and Kimberley interviewed me by phone. At the end of the call she said she would get back to me. A second e-mail followed, saying, "I think I will ask my boss to hire you." Several more e-mails arrived, and now I've been here in this heaven on earth they call Guilin for more than a month.

In China there is a saying, "Better than being an Immortal is to be a human living in Guilin." This is the home of the Karst mountains, the subject of many Chinese paintings for the last thousand years or so. Poets have written many lines inspired by their travels here.

The air is clean and pure. On a warm day the scent from the many sweet osmanthus that grow here delights the senses. The mountains are often partially shrouded in mist, giving them that mysterious appearance they have in Chinese paintings. There are times on campus, where we have several of these pointed peaks, that I walk around feeling as if I'm in the midst of one of those paintings.

When I look back on what happened, I realize I was holding on to the belief I was too old and too ill to be able to follow my passions. The Passion Test somehow added the clarity and energy I needed to transcend those beliefs so that I could create this passion in my life. Now, instead of living out my life wishing for what might have been, I am immersed in living the life of my dreams.

We recently got an update from Otto. After a month in Guilin he got news that a close relative was diagnosed with a bone tumor. Like Janet, his top passions shifted immediately. It became much more important to come home and be with family than to stay in Guilin, so he returned. He had a wonderful time in Guilin, and he is now with those he loves most.

As we've said before, you can't know where your passions will lead you. You can know that by staying open and aligned with your passions, you will stay connected to the things that matter most to you.

As we were completing this edition of the book, we had to go to Chicago from Iowa to give one of our Passion Test Certification courses. Janet had the thought that if we took the Amtrak train instead of driving our car, we would have more time to write.

Instead, on the train, we met a crusty old sailor nicknamed Krunch. His skin was brown and weathered. He was gruff and not at all talkative at first. If you didn't have Janet Attwood's inquisitive nature and award-winning persistence, you would have missed the wonderful story she pried out of him about what can happen when you stay open. Sometimes your passions will come walking right up to you. It's just a matter of saying yes!

Krunch's real name is Robert "Bobby" Duckstein. Here's his story of how his passion found him:

> One day in 1974, I opened up a *National Geographic* magazine and there was a photograph of three Polynesian women. I still have a copy of that magazine.
> I don't remember the caption verbatim, but it was something like, "These women of Polynesian and European an-

cestry from Tahiti can dispute the beauty of any place they are assigned." Being young and dumb and full of *cojones*, that's where I wanted to go. But I knew you either had to go by boat, and I didn't know how to spell the word *boat*, or you had to fly, and I didn't have any money. So I just shelved the idea and forgot about it, but I couldn't stop thinking about those women because they were gorgeous, drop-dead gorgeous.

I ended up in New Mexico living in a teepee—me with a bunch of people. That's the short version.

One day four of us, my friend and two women and I, decided we were going to drive from Santa Fe to Juárez, Mexico, to buy tequila and that's what we did. We got in a truck and drove the 350 miles to Juárez and got rip-roaring drunk. The next thing I remember is falling out of a truck at 45 miles an hour and waking up in a cornfield. Nothing got hurt so I got back in the truck.

My next memory was waking up in Mazatlán, which is 1,200 miles from Juarez. We were all sitting in this restaurant when this Swedish fellow walks in, looks at us, and he goes, "Ya, I need help to sail my boat to Tahiti."

I was still a little hungover 'cause not much time had passed, and my friend looks at me and he says, "Bobby, if you don't do this now, you're never going to get a chance like this ever again."

So I turned to the Swede and I said, "I've never been on a boat before. I'm scared—less of drowning. I don't have any money, don't like sharks, can't swim, don't know anything about boats, but I'll go with you."

He says to me, "You're just the guy I want." "Why's that?" I asked and he says, "Because you can't tell me what to do."

As I walked out of the restaurant, I turned around and looked at the name of this restaurant. It was called the Aloha Café. How appropriate. That restaurant is still in Mazatlán today.

So fifteen minutes later I was on board Eagle's boat. Most kids want to be a doctor or a lawyer or a judge or a pilot, but I had no idea what I wanted to do. But from the moment we set sail, with the stars and the ocean, I said this is where I belong.

We went from Mazatlán to the Cocos Islands to the Galápagos to the Marquesas to Tahiti to the Cook Islands to Hawaii and back to Vancouver, Canada. I went away for the weekend. I came home eleven months later, and I spent most of the next three years with this guy getting into trouble all over the Pacific.

Today I work on large training ships, sailing vessels, schooners, and such. Most people think they look like pirate ships because they were made famous in those days. We take college students out for a month at a time. We take high school and middle school students out for a week at a time, or two or three days at a time, sometimes just for three hours and depending on what boat I'm working on there's a different program for each boat.

On the boat I just left, we do an 1812 program about the War of 1812. On the previous boat, the *Lady Washington*, we did history classes on the merchant men of the West Coast and the Spanish missions. We talk about the evolution of trade and why these boats were so important.

I love what I do. Some people say they want to live their dream. I say, I am the dream.

We loved Krunch's story because it shows what can happen when you stay open. The most unexpected, and wonderful, things can happen when you're able to let go of your ideas of what you can do.

Speed Limits on the Cosmic Highway

As CEO, Stephen M. R. Covey helped build the Covey Leadership Center into the largest consultancy of its kind and orchestrated its multimillion-dollar merger with Franklin Quest to create the publicly traded company FranklinCovey. In a moment you will read our interview with Stephen, as he talks about the subject of his latest book, *The Speed of Trust*, and how it affects every relationship in your life. First let's talk about your journey down the cosmic highway.

**The speed you travel on the road of life is
determined by the beliefs and concepts you hold.**

How long it takes you to fulfill your dreams is directly related to your beliefs. There was a time when Donald Trump almost went bankrupt, yet not long after he was a billionaire again. How is that possible?

If you made a million dollars in the next year, would you consider that a good year? What do you think Donald Trump would think if he only made a million dollars in the coming year? He'd think the year was a huge failure, wouldn't he? The key difference between you and Donald is the beliefs you hold.

In the last chapter we said there are only three things (which are really one thing) that can keep you from living a passionate life:

- False ideas
- False concepts
- False beliefs

What are the beliefs you hold about your ability to live your passions? Here are some we hear:

- I can't live my passions because I have to support my family.
- I can't make money from the things I'm passionate about.
- I don't have the skills to be really successful.
- I'm too old. It's too late for me.
- I'm too young. I don't have enough experience.
- I'm too _____ (you fill in the blank: weak, afraid, tall, short, fat, skinny . . .).
- I don't know enough.
- I'm not outgoing enough.
- I'm not _____ enough. (You fill in the blank—this is really "I'm not enough.")

No matter who you are, no matter what your situation, no matter what your handicaps, thinking that these things prevent you from living your passions are all simply false ideas, false concepts, and false beliefs. These are thoughts you hold that are simply not true. They are out of sync with reality.

**When you feel truly passionate about something,
you will always have the ability
to create it in your life.**

Think about it. Is it true you can't make money from living your passions? Would you ever believe that someone could make money from a passion for sitting around and chatting with people? Oprah Winfrey seems to have done pretty well with that one.

What about a passion for baking cookies? Mrs. Fields seems to have managed that one. How about a passion for watching movies? Roger Ebert figured that one out.

You don't have the skills? Do you know any famous musicians with terrible singing voices (we don't want to insult anyone, but we're sure you can think of as many as we can). Ever heard any stories about CEOs who were once mail room clerks? Did you know that Albert Einstein flunked most of his courses in school? How about Abraham Lincoln? He lost his mother, lost election after election, lost his money, failed at business, and if you were just looking at the things that didn't work out, appeared to be a failure most of his life until he was elected president of the United States.

You're too old? Do you know that most millionaires are made after the age of fifty-five? While he cooked chicken for years, it wasn't until Colonel Sanders was sixty-two that he started Kentucky Fried Chicken. And you've already read the story of Otto at the beginning of this chapter.

No matter what limiting belief you hold, there is evidence in the world to the contrary. Even if there is no one who has ever done what you are passionate about doing, there is abundant evidence of people who have been successful doing what others thought was impossible.

You are powerful beyond your imagination. As we said in part 1, you have created your life, and the good news is, if you don't like it you can change it. Remember this mantra?

**Your life is created first in your mind
then in the world.**

As long as you believe you can't, you won't be able to. As long as you believe it's not possible, it won't be possible for you. As long as you believe it's too hard, it will be too hard for you.

So does that mean the opposite is also true, that as long as you believe you can, you'll be able to? Yes, and it's not so simple, because our beliefs run deep. You can say, "I can do it," and still not believe you can, deep inside. This is why affirmations often don't produce the results we'd like them to.

But do you remember when we talked about the power of asking questions? When you ask your mind a question, it will search for an answer. If you haven't believed you can live your passions, then ask yourself, what evidence can I find that maybe I *can* live my passions?

Keep looking for evidence until you can feel it deep inside: "Of course I can do it. Look at all the other people who have done it, look at all the evidence there is that this is possible." This is your first and most important task in living your passions— discover the evidence you need in order to believe you can do it.

This is one of the reasons we host the "Passions Series" at *Healthy Wealthy nWise*. When you hear how John Assaraf started as a gang member, or how Neale Donald Walsch lived in the streets for some time, or how David Lynch discovered his passion by seeing his friend's father making a living as an artist, or how Mark Victor Hansen survived bankruptcy, it helps you believe that if they can do it, you can do it too.

Traveling at the Speed of Thought

It was 1999 when a friend convinced Janet to attend a lecture that provided the most powerful tool we have experienced for changing false beliefs:

> I didn't know what to expect, but Radhika said it would be amazing, so I went. A beautiful, silver-haired woman sat at the front of the room.
>
> "I spent ten years in deep depression," she said. "It got to the point that I hardly left my bedroom. My children tiptoed past my door, hoping I wouldn't scream at them. I weighed over two hundred pounds. Sometimes two weeks would go by before I could get myself to brush my teeth or bathe. Day after day I would lie in bed with such self-hatred, so hopeless and suicidal that I was beyond despair.
>
> "Finally, it got so bad that I checked myself into a halfway house for women with eating disorders. It was the only place my insurance would pay for. The other women were so frightened of me that I was put up in the attic, away from the other residents. I felt so worthless that I didn't even believe I deserved to sleep in a bed, so I slept on the floor.
>
> "Then one morning, about a week later, a cockroach crawled over my foot, and I opened my eyes. All my rage, all the thoughts that had been troubling me, my

whole world was gone, and in its place was a joy I can't begin to describe. I felt that if my joy were told, it would blow the roof off the halfway house—off the whole planet. I still feel that way.

"I realized at that moment that when I believed my thoughts I suffered, but when I didn't believe them I didn't suffer, and this is true for every human being. Freedom is as simple as that. I found that suffering is optional. I found a joy within me that has never disappeared, not for a single moment. That joy is in everyone, always."

Byron Katie paused, before continuing. "We don't suffer because of what happens, we suffer because of our thoughts about what happens. Reality is neither good nor bad. Only our thoughts make it good or bad. When you question your stressful thoughts, you realize they have no basis in reality. Eventually, you come to see that everything outside you is a reflection of your own thinking. You are the storyteller, the projector of all stories, and the world is the projected image of your thoughts.

"Since the beginning of time, people have been trying to change the world so they can be happy. This hasn't ever worked, because it approaches the problem backward. What I bring people is a way to change the projector—mind—rather than the projected. It's like when there's a piece of lint on a projector's lens. We think there's a flaw on the screen, and we try to change this person and that person—whoever the flaw appears to be on next. But it's futile to try to change the projected images. Once we realize where the lint is, we can clear the lens itself. This is the end of suffering, and the beginning of a little joy in paradise."

After the lecture, Radhika invited me to come have lunch with Katie and some of the people who were with her. I came a little late and the only seat was right next to Katie.

As I was introduced to her, Katie turned to me with a radiant smile and said, "Hello, angel, what do you do?" I replied that I was in charge of marketing for a large company in town. I was a little surprised by Katie's next question, "Are you good at what you do?" she asked.

Without missing a beat, I said, "I'm the best!" After all, I had been the top account executive for five years, was currently managing the marketing division at Books Are Fun, and we were having a record year.

Since she had met me only minutes before, Katie's next comment was even more surprising. "I'd like you to come and do my marketing. You can live at my home in Manhattan Beach. Will you come?"

I was so drawn to this woman, and part of me wanted to say yes immediately. Another part of me was thinking about my house, my three golden retrievers, my two cats, and how could I ever make such a radical change in my life?

When I went home I just couldn't stop thinking about this amazing woman. Finally, I called Chris, who was living in North Carolina, and told him the story of my remarkable meeting. "Will you come with me to see her in DC and Boston? I can't make this decision by myself."

After some cajoling, Chris finally agreed to make the trip with me. We spent a magical weekend with Katie in Washington DC, and then flew to Boston where she was presenting in Cambridge.

I use the word *presenting* loosely, because Katie

doesn't really present. She sits with a volunteer who has an issue they want to investigate, and then Katie takes the person through the process of internal questioning she simply calls The Work. The Work is summarized in Katie's little jingle: "Judge your neighbor, write it down, ask four questions, and turn it around."

I will never forget one particular interaction at the event in Cambridge. Katie invited the audience to think of some social issue they felt was just terrible. A woman raised her hand and came up to the front.

Katie greeted her warmly. "Hello, sweetheart. What is it that's troubling you?"

"There shouldn't be starving children in the world," the woman replied.

"There shouldn't be starving children in the world—is that true?" Katie asked. "What's the reality? Are there?"

"Well, of course there are," the woman replied.

"So can you absolutely know that there shouldn't be starving children in the world?"

"Yes," the woman said.

"When you argue with reality, you lose—but only 100 percent of the time," Katie said, addressing the audience. Then, turning back to the woman, "How do you react when you believe that there shouldn't be starving children in the world, and there are?"

"I hate Americans for not feeding the children. I can't understand how with all their wealth and abundance they can allow this to continue. I get so enraged. Sometimes I want to kill them," the woman answered.

"How else do you react when you believe that thought?" Katie said.

"I feel completely helpless. I feel confused. I think I should be doing something, but I don't know what to do. I get depressed. Sometimes I can't bear it," the woman said, overtaken by emotion.

Katie asked her, "Can you think of one peaceful reason to keep this thought that there shouldn't be starving children in the world?" To the audience, Katie said, "This is not about condoning starvation. This is about ending suffering on this planet, and we end it one person at a time, beginning with you. When you question your thinking, and find what is really true for you, you have the clarity to do something about a problem, if you choose to, rather than making yourself miserable thinking about it."

Katie directed the question again to the woman. "So, honey, can you think of one peaceful reason to hold on to this painful, angry thought, that there shouldn't be starving children in the world?"

The woman replied, "No. No, that thought only drives me crazy."

"Who would you be without the thought?" Katie asked.

"Well, I'd be a lot happier. I wouldn't be worried all the time. I'd feel a whole lot better."

"Good," Katie said. "So with the thought, stress. And without the thought, a lot happier. So it isn't the starving children that are causing you to suffer, it's your thought about them. Can you hear this, sweetheart?"

"I think so," the woman said.

"And without the thought, you sound like someone who is really in a position to help solve the problem. Now turn the thought around. What is the exact opposite of this thought, that there shouldn't be starving children in the world?"

"There should be starving children in the world?" the woman asked hesitantly.

"Can you find one example of how that could be true?" Katie asked.

The woman thought for a few moments, then said, "No."

Katie said, "There should be starving children in the world because, whether we like it or not, there are. Our shoulds and shouldn'ts have no effect on the situation. What is, is. I have come to see that God is everything and God is good. When we are able to love what is, we can stop torturing ourselves and act with freedom. Love is action. It's clear, it's kind, it's effortless, and it's irresistible."

Katie turned to the woman and asked, "What's another turnaround, honey? Begin with 'I shouldn't . . .'"

The woman made a quizzical face and then said, "I shouldn't be starving?" As soon as she asked this question, she began sobbing.

Katie took the woman in her arms and held her until the sobbing had stopped. Then she asked, "What is it, angel?"

The woman replied through her tears, "I am anorexic, and I just realized that this is what I've been doing. I've been starving myself."

Katie kindly said, "Yes, sweetheart, it's time to feed yourself." And to the audience she said, "This is what we do. We take our stressful thoughts and project them out onto the world. When you investigate your thinking, you'll discover that it's not about anyone else. It's all about you. If you have judgments about someone else, then write them down, question them, and turn them around. Be your own teacher. Do what it is you want them to do. If you want the world to be fed, begin by feeding yourself."

Katie gave the woman a hug and said, "Thank you for your courage, angel. It takes courage to do this Work, to question what we so firmly believe is true. You are amazing. Do you know what you need to do now?"

"Yes, Katie. I know exactly what I need to do. Thank you so much."

As you can imagine, both Chris and I were profoundly moved. We went with Katie to the house where she was staying and talked with her for some time about her offer for me to come work for her. Chris was so deeply touched by the experience of being with Katie that we both ended up working for her. While I did help Katie with her marketing, the funny thing is that I never made the move to California. But a few months later, Chris moved out there—lock, stock, and barrel—and spent almost a year living and working at Katie's house in Manhattan Beach.

The Work of Byron Katie is one of the most powerful tools we have discovered for undoing your limiting beliefs. Katie makes The Work available without charge. In fact, you can go to her Website, read a complete explanation of The Work, hear audio recordings of Katie taking people through The Work, and then download a Worksheet to help you do The Work yourself.

As you investigate the thoughts that make you feel afraid, that make you feel unworthy, that make you feel unlovable, you will discover something new growing in you: trust.

Your speed on the cosmic highway is directly related to

your ability to trust in the benevolence of the universe. What does that mean?

Life is designed for your joy. It is designed to allow you to experience ever-increasing fulfillment. And if you're saying, "Well, that's not my experience ...," then you may be interested to know that this was the common theme of every one of the Saints Janet interviewed in her trek around India and Nepal. And it was very obvious that this is their direct experience.

So what does it take for it to become your direct experience?

Change your mind about what you choose to experience in your life.

What feels better, to believe that you are alone in the world, that you have to struggle and strain to get ahead, or to believe you are surrounded by a benevolent universe that is constantly giving you gifts? What feels better, to believe life is hard and difficult and disappointing, or to believe that life is an adventure, an opportunity to explore your own true nature?

What you believe, you will create. Old beliefs can sometimes be hard to change. That's why we have shared The Work of Byron Katie with you.

When you begin to look for evidence that life is ultimately kind, you will start to find that evidence. When you begin to look for reasons to believe that every experience is a blessing, you will start to find those reasons.

As you begin to embrace the idea that life is here for your joy, that every moment is a gift, showing you the path to fulfillment, you will discover magic happening in your life just as Julia Ghavami did.

In October 2006 I attended a seminar where Janet Attwood took us through The Passion Test. At the time I was struggling because my marriage seemed to be coming apart. At the same time I was looking for a way to bring in an income to sustain myself and still homeschool my children. My health had been strained for many years and was taxing my daily life. I knew what I wanted and had no idea how to get there.

As I sat in the seminar going through The Passion Test with Janet, writing down what I really wanted to see in my life, I realized that I wasn't living my passions.

My top five passions were:

1. enjoying an awesome relationship with my husband
2. powerfully homeschooling my children
3. living a life of abundant health
4. having multiple streams of income
5. being a public speaker and motivating others

My friend asked me why I wasn't doing public speaking. I said I didn't have a book so who would want to hear from me. At that time Janet said we could become Passion Test facilitators and my friend said, here's your book.

I left the event truly focused on what I loved, and I knew for the first time in my life that my passions would unfold before me. Physically, mentally, spiritually, and emotionally it was all clicking. An amazing transformation had happened in me. I realized I wasn't living the life I wanted to live because my focus was sidetracked by daily life. The demands on me were great in so many areas. Some things were aligned with my passions and some were not. I needed to make the choices for my passions, and I knew God would make sure that *all* would come into fruition. In other words, I got it!

I am now a paid Passion Test facilitator. I am a speaker for another company through which I have made more than fifty thousand dollars in the last four months. I am also getting paid to help others with BEST—Morter Health System's Bioenergetic Synchronization Technique—which has transformed my health in ways that have amazed me. I'm earning multiple streams of income, and I am a motivational speaker and trainer.

My boys are getting a fabulous and more focused education. I have hired a tutor for the areas I was struggling in. More than the fact that they are doing better with their schoolwork, my number one focus is the hearts of the young men I am raising.

My boys have done The Passion Test as well. I am helping them focus on what they want in their lives and teaching them to dream about possibilities for their future and their daily lives. They are motivated because they have something to work toward even if it may change daily. They have a vision at ages nine and eleven and are encouraged to create.

Finally, I had no idea how my marriage could be saved. I had struggled for many years, focused on trying to fix it so that my children could grow up in a two-parent home. It got far worse before it ever got better. Then one day, out of nowhere, my husband came to me with healing words and a transformed heart that changed our whole relationship. Ours is now an awesome, loving marriage that is stronger

than ever before. I look forward to spending the rest of my
life with him.

I have seen my life change before my eyes, and The Passion Test gave me the tools to focus on what I truly want in
my life and then stay open to what God brought in. He gave
me my heart's desire and what he had always intended me
to have.

You live in a universe designed to deliver the greatest possible
joy, the greatest possible experience of fulfillment—when you
are open to receive it.

You can never know how the gifts in your life will appear.
Some of your most significant trials may turn out to be the
greatest blessings. But here's one thing you can count on:

**As your trust that things will work out well grows,
the speed with which you manifest your dreams
will increase dramatically.**

Trust is fundamental. It is the key to success in business, success in relationships, and success in life. In the following interview, Stephen M. R. Covey shares some very practical points
about how you can increase the trust in your life.

Stephen M. R. Covey

*Stephen M. R. Covey was responsible for the strategy that
propelled his father's book, Dr. Stephen R. Covey's The 7*

Habits of Highly Effective People, *to become one of the top two most influential business books of the twentieth century, according to* CEO *magazine.*

As CEO of Covey Leadership Center, he transformed that company into the largest leadership development firm in the world. During his tenure, Covey Leadership Center's revenues grew to $112 million. Profits increased twelve times during the same period. When he took over, the company was valued at $2.4 million. Within three years he had raised shareholder value to $160 million and orchestrated a merger with Franklin Quest to create FranklinCovey.

He has now cofounded his own consultancy firm, CoveyLink, and is recognized as a leading authority in creating high-trust, high-performance organizations. His book, The Speed of Trust, *represents a major contribution to the understanding of one of the key components of high-performance individuals and organizations.*

"As I was thinking about a new direction in my life, my father posed a great little statement that got me thinking. He said, 'Stephen, that's great if you want to do real estate. Nothing wrong with that. It's exciting, it's fun, you're good at it. But do you want to spend your life building buildings or building souls?'

"It struck me that there's nothing wrong with building buildings, it's exciting work, but the chance to have an impact on people, to really help people create and develop their own potential and to manifest it in their lives was very appealing. So I said, 'You know what? I want to focus on building souls and building people, and the organizations in which they reside.'

"I made that move then and ran with it for many, many years, and helped build Covey Leadership Center into the largest leadership development company in the world. After the merger with Franklin Quest to form FranklinCovey, I stayed on with the new company, but then, over time, decided I wanted to do some new things.

"So I set out on a number of different entrepreneurial ventures. Again, all of them were very exciting and interesting, very stimulating intellectually, but I recognized, after having experienced the work I'd been doing with Covey Leadership Center for so many years, that something was missing.

"What was missing was that I needed to have all of my needs met. I wanted the work I was doing to matter, to make a difference—not just to make money and not just to have fun and not just to develop my talents. All of those things were very important to me, but I also wanted to make a difference in people's lives.

"So it's by learning through living that I've come around to understand, follow, and run with what I consider to be my passions. I spent some time exploring options, even before Covey, but then I had this long period of time at Covey, and it was terrific. I was excited to try some new things. However, as I did, I found I definitely lacked variety.

"I had to return to something with a spiritual dimension— some meaning, some purpose, some passion. My passion. I found that was vital. Having experienced the difference, I had to return to what I knew, so now I'm back in the world of ideas and ways to help people.

"Over the last seventeen years, I've been involved heavily in the idea of releasing human potential, releasing talent. I've not been just someone talking about it. I've actually helped to build something and do something. It became very clear to me, during that time, that trust is the highest form of human motivation. It provides a motivation that is different in kind from anything else.

"I began to recognize this as I looked back at some of the early struggles we had at Covey Leadership Center. Our issue was not whether we had a good idea in the marketplace. We did. We also had a lot of client appeal and attraction to what we were doing, but we were losing a lot of value by not building an organization that had trust in all its relationships.

"We had trust with our key players, but we had not built an organization with the level of trust we needed yet. I came across this great quote by Francis Fukuyama, which really had an impact on me. It created a passion for this topic. The quote was, 'Widespread distrust in a society . . . imposes a kind of tax on all forms of economic activity, a tax that high-trust societies do not have to pay.'

"I began to think, 'Well, not only is it in a society, but widespread distrust in an organization imposes a tax on everything.' Widespread distrust in a relationship imposes a tax on every activity that high-trust organizations, high-trust relationships don't have to pay. While our trust level was not extremely low, because we had great people and we were doing good things, nonetheless, we felt there was a gap there. We were paying a tax, and any tax was too much.

"So I began to focus on how to eliminate this low-trust tax and instead give the opposite of a tax, which is a dividend. That was the whole notion of trust affecting everything else— everything around us in our organizations and our relationships. It began to be something I put more energy into, and I saw that it was something widely misunderstood in business, widely misunderstood in life, and that could have a profound impact.

"For example, let's take the tragedy that happened to the United States a few years ago, with the 9/11 activity, when terrible terrorist acts took place. After September 11, trust in our entire air transportation system, the airline system in the United States, went down quite a bit, because people began to worry about the safety of traveling.

"It was both, 'There are people out to get us' (terrorists have an agenda), and also, 'Is our system set up to catch them? Is it trustworthy? Is it capable of catching this?' So trust went down.

"Trust always affects two measures every time. Whether it be low trust or high trust, it affects two measures. They are: speed and cost. When trust goes down, there's a tax. That tax is seen in slower speed (things take longer) and higher cost (things cost more).

"Here's an illustration. Warren Buffett, the CEO of Berkshire Hathaway, is well known. He always writes a management letter every year with his annual report. His management letters are studied widely in business schools around the country and the world.

"Some time ago, in his management letter, he talked about the big acquisition of the McLane distribution company from Wal-Mart.

"Now, Berkshire Hathaway is public, Wal-Mart is public, so these are two public companies. They meet all the requirements of the public marketplace, all the scrutiny, etc. But this deal took place in a two-hour meeting, and then twenty-nine days later Wal-Mart had its money from Berkshire Hathaway—a $23 billion transaction.

"Berkshire Hathaway did no due diligence, and Warren Buffett said, 'In essence, I trusted Wal-Mart, I trusted the people I worked with. I knew everything would be in exactly the order they said it would be, and it was.'

"In most mergers of this size, we're talking several months, if not six, eight, ten, twelve months to close a deal like this, with armies and teams of accountants, CPAs, attorneys, etc. that come in and do all kinds of due diligence to verify, to validate. It costs a lot and it takes a lot of time.

"But the idea of the speed of trust is literally both speed in terms of the actual time in which you can do things and also speed as a metaphor, to mean benefits, results, dividends that are abundant—the fruits of high trust, the speed at which you're able to move, and the benefits produced. In this case, a deal was done in twenty-nine days, start to finish, out of a two-hour meeting, because there was high trust in the relationship between the principals of these companies.

"What an amazing ability to move, and with speed. In low-trust relationships, the amount of time and energy that's wasted and spent on other agendas is extraordinary. It's characteristic of low trust, whereas high trust is the opposite. Things are open, they're on the table, there's no hidden agenda. It's transparent, and you're able to move with extraordinary speed.

"Trust profoundly impacts our own missions and destinies because we live today in an interdependent, interconnected world. I'm not just talking about being wired and the fact that it's a wired world and we're all connected that way. We are wired, and everything affects everything else.

"It's an ecosystem: it's very interdependent, and there's very little that's truly isolated. It's a global economy, and changes taking place in India affect things in the United States and vice versa and all over the world. In this interdependent world there is a premium on working with people, with multiple stakeholders. By stakeholders I mean those with a stake in your success and what you're doing, what you're all about. So these are customers, investors, suppliers, shareholders, employees, influencers, people you work with, people you want to influence.

"Relationships are at the heart of interdependence. Trust is truly the key, the glue that makes relationships work. It increases speed and decreases cost, time and again. Relationships are at the heart of this interdependent world we're living in, and that's just the reality—we are living in this world.

"So in most cases of people looking to live out and express their own unique voice, it is not isolated in them. It might be that they want to impact, affect, work with, or influence other people, in some way and fashion in their life, and the key to that interdependence is relationships. The key to relationships is trust, building relationships at the speed of trust, and carrying them out that way.

"Carl Rogers said, 'That which is most personal is most general.' So all of us have experienced relationships of low trust and relationships of high trust. We all know them, so it applies across the board. We get it. Once we frame it this way, we can say, 'I get it. Help me now improve it.'

The process of building trust is an interesting one, but it begins with yourself, with what I call self-trust, and with your own credibility, your own trustworthiness. If you think about it, it's hard to establish trust with others if you can't trust yourself. Trustworthiness is really the foundation upon which relationships or trust are built.

"I call this self-trust, building individual credibility. Basically, there are two dimensions to how trust works and how this individual credibility works. First, there's character; second, there's competence. Both are vital to building trust with others. Both are vital to building self-trust.

"Character, as it relates to trust, is the one we understand the most. When we think of trust, most of us put it in the 'softer' terms of character. It includes our integrity and the like. That's vital—the character component is vital because we need to have integrity to be trusted, to trust ourselves, as well as to have others trust us.

"Also, we need to have competence. If you think about it, you don't trust someone if they're not competent to deliver results. You might trust their heart, their character, but you wouldn't trust them to get a job done.

"My wife trusts me; I trust my wife. I care for her, I'm honest with her, and she with me. She recently had to have some surgery, and you know what? As much as I trust her and she trusts me, she did not ask me to do the surgery, and it's obvious why not! I'm not a doctor. I don't have any competence in the medical profession, and so she wouldn't trust me in that, and yet she would trust me to help raise a family with her.

"So, both character and competence are vital, and it just depends on what you need to accomplish, what you need to do. Character is a constant, and the competency needed is very task-oriented or job-oriented, very situation-oriented, but both are vital—character and competency.

"It's in our homes and our families that most people first learn about trust. We start with a basic, implicit understanding of it, and we extend trust rather easily, usually as young children.

"I was very blessed and fortunate to grow up in a home where both my father and mother were great models of this. Both in teaching us integrity and teaching us the idea of making a difference and making a contribution in life, but also the way they interacted with us really did build trust.

"A popular story, for those who have read my father's book, *The 7 Habits of Highly Effective People*, is the story of 'Green and Clean.' It's the story of my father training me (I was a young child at the time, about seven years old) how to take care of the yard and how to make sure the yard was green and clean.

"That was my job. I could do it however I wanted. My father recommended I might turn on the sprinklers because that would help, but he said, 'If you want to use buckets and just pour water on the lawn, you can do that too.' He taught me that the idea was—you achieve results.

"The result here was that I wanted a green yard, and clean. It was up to me how to do it, but he gave me some good ideas on how to do it. At the time, I was rather young. My father uses this story to talk about how he was teaching stewardship delegation and he was delegating results, and the responsibility to take care of that. And it is true. It was stewardship delegation.

"My father also talked about this in terms of being a win-win agreement, that he was teaching me that if I did this, here was my win, and here was his win, and it was a win-win agreement.

"Do you know what? What I remember, because I was just

seven years old, was that I felt trusted. I felt an extension of trust from my father to me, to take care of this yard. I was too young to care about money at the time. That didn't motivate me.

"What motivated me was that I didn't want to let my father down. I wanted to come through. I wanted to show I was capable and responsible for doing what he thought I was doing. What he was giving me was the responsibility to take care of something. I felt trust. That motivated me. He extended it to me. It inspired me and built in me a sense of responsibility and stewardship and integrity that has stayed with me throughout my life. Now I'm trying to pass it on to my children.

"We clearly learn this in the home, both the character dimension of trust and also how to extend trust, how to expand trust, and how to be a good model of this trust. The modeling is so important.

"Example comes first, then relationship, then teaching, because example is seen, relationship is felt, teaching is heard. People tend not to hear until they see and feel, and that's what happened with me. I saw and I felt in my home. Then that enabled me to hear, because of what I was seeing and feeling.

"There's the whole mind-set you go into business and into life with, and it is, 'Can I trust other people or not, and do I want to trust other people or not?' People want to be trusted. It brings out the best in them. It's an extraordinary form of motivation.

"When people don't feel trusted, when they don't feel their boss trusts them, then it is a demotivator and is discouraging. Then they are more apt to leave and go somewhere else and do other things. It doesn't bring out the best in them at all. It doesn't bring out their passion and their talents and creativity.

"It's very important to have a desire and intent to seek the trust of other people. You just don't want to get ahead of yourself with extending too much trust beyond their competence or their character.

"Business is better when you release people and their talents and capabilities. I remember Robert Galvin Jr., the CEO of Motorola, who took over from his father. He did a great job and he said he was asked this question: 'People ask me how I had the interest and the zeal to hang in there and do what I've done. I say, "Because my father treated me with very stern discipline. He trusted me. I'm stuck. I've got to see the trust through. He trusted me. I trust other people, and they do the job."'

"So, the whole idea was that trust is a great form of motivation—of releasing talent, energy, passion—of releasing your own energy and passion by being trusted and also by extending trust to other people.

"You just want to make sure you do it with wisdom and by understanding character and competence. You've got to match them up. What's the competence needed to perform the task at hand?

"The need is to first start with yourself and be credible, to focus on your character, your competence. Learn how to interact in ways that build the trust within your relationship, and learn how to avoid the ways that destroy it.

"Let me give two simple examples that everyone can apply today, tonight, or tomorrow. Here are two ways you can immediately begin to increase trust in a relationship. The first is to create more transparency in any given relationship. By transparency, I mean openness. It means to tell the truth in a way that other people can validate, can verify.

"The opposite of transparency is having a hidden agenda because then you're not open. There you've got something hidden, and in most cases people sense it; they feel it. They don't know what it is, but they distrust what you're doing because they question what your real agenda or motive is.

"Instead, be transparent. Be open. 'Here's what I'm trying to do. Here's why.' Companies that do this, leaders who do this, experience far greater results. Individuals who do this in relationships get better results because it opens things up, and they realize, 'Here's your agenda. Your agenda is on the table.' It's open, it's clear.

"Recently, there's been a big challenge with some charities, where people are asking, 'What are you using your money for?' If people are going to donate money to charities, you can't lose that trust. The best way to keep it is to become transparent: open up your books, open up what you're doing with the money. If people are questioning what you're doing, open it up.

"Make sure you're worthy of their trust by doing the right things with the money. But, if trust is low, remember people don't trust what they can't see. So let them see it, open it up. I know a lot of companies have opened up their financial books and let people see the financials because the very process of doing that is a great demonstration of trust.

"You need to apply this in your own situation. If you're trying to build trust in a particular relationship, ask, 'How can I be more open, more transparent so others can see what I'm really trying to do—my intent, my motive?' In the very process of doing that, you challenge yourself because maybe you're not being open. Maybe you do have a hidden agenda. If you do, you're not going to be building trust. People will sense it. Instead, be open, be clear, be transparent, and you'll be amazed at the immediate impact it can have.

"Let me give you the second example. You can take issues head-on. Confront reality, take these issues head-on, even things that are so-called undiscussable, because so often what happens is that we skirt issues. We avoid them, we run from them, especially for a leader within a company or within a team.

"If there are things everyone's talking about, but we're not talking about it as a team, it's the undiscussable. Yet everyone discusses it behind the scenes. Ignoring it only decreases trust because it signifies one of two things: either you're not open and honest with people, which is not being transparent, or you're clueless, you don't understand. That's not good either.

"So which is it? Both are bad. Instead of ignoring it and skirting it, take it head-on, tee it up. Say, 'I understand we've got this issue. Let's discuss this.' Because it's being discussed anyway, with or without you. Why not have it be with you?

"I had this situation, after the merger of Franklin and Covey. We had a group in which we were really struggling with building trust. All mergers are tough; the parties struggle with trust issues, and we did too. Here I was, the president of this unit, trying to build trust. I had a one-hour speech with a team of consultants. We were supposed to talk about strategy.

"You know what? I could see and sense no one really wanted to talk about strategy. They wanted to talk about a whole host of merger issues that were dividing the company culture and dividing us from bringing our companies together. I decided, you know, I can talk about strategy, play it safe, and probably get nowhere. Or I could really open it up and say, 'What would you really like to talk about?' I knew they wanted to talk about these things, and I could then make it safe for them by bringing some of these issues up myself.

"So I did. I opened it up and said, 'I sense from private conversations that some of you would really like to talk about our process of integrating these companies. Who's making the decisions? Whose philosophy is winning out? How are we going about doing this? Which physical facilities are we going to keep and which not? Is that right?'

"Everyone said, 'Yeah! We really would like to talk about that.' Then they opened up and they began to ask real tough questions. Rather than skirt them, I took them head-on. The net effect was that I had people afterward say to me, 'You know what? We built more trust in one day than we had in the prior year. I appreciate your being open and honest and taking these issues head-on.'

"I didn't have answers for everything, and I'm not giving myself as a great model of this. I struggled too, but I've learned that creating transparency and confronting reality are two quick, easy ways any of us can increase the trust in relationships with our teams and organizations.

"I'm excited about this work I'm doing on trust, and I'm building what I call a 'trust practice.' The whole idea is to focus on helping individuals and organizations build trust, create trust, grow trust with all stakeholders they interact with, in order to improve business results and their own personal results in their lives. Part of this includes my book, *The Speed of Trust.*

"It's much more than just business, it's relationships and so much more—leadership at the speed of trust. This has excited me. I'm taking on a topic that has been very much misunderstood and almost even maligned by some. There are so many myths around trust.

"It's seen as soft, it's seen as slow, as nebulous. I saw something this week that said, 'Can you teach trust?' I want to emphatically answer: Absolutely! Trust can be taught, it can be learned, it can be implemented, it can be grown, it can be measured, it can be applied in an organization, and it can and should be an explicit objective of every relationship, of every organization.

"It's there whether you're aware of it or not. Either you have trust or you don't. If you have it, you'll get a dividend. It will pay results to you in countless ways. You'll see it in speed and cost. If trust is low, you're also paying a price; you're paying a tax that will be manifest in speed and cost, and is happening whether you believe it or buy it.

"It's inevitable that low trust means low speed, high cost.

"The final thought or idea I'd leave with your readers is simply this: I predict the ability to create, grow, extend, and restore trust with all stakeholders will become the key leadership competency of the twenty-first century. And I mean that seriously—more than strategy, more than vision, more than all these different things.

"The reason I say that—it's a pretty bold prediction to say it's going to be the key leadership competency, the ability to create, grow, extend, and restore trust with all stakeholders—is that we're in a knowledge-worker economy, where relationships are the key. Low trust is everywhere in our society and our organizations, it's all around us.

"There's an extraordinary high cost of this low trust, which we see manifest in both speed and cost, and trust affects everything else we do. It affects our strategy, our execution, our innovation, our communication. Every dimension in a company, in a relationship, is affected by trust, its presence or absence.

"Therefore, as we increase the trust in our organizations and our relationships, we experience this multiplicative effect, this multiplier that increases rather than taxes what we're doing. It increases the communication rather than taxes it. It increases our ability to execute rather than discounting our ability to execute, and it affects every dimension, every aspect of this.

"Begin creating more trusting relationships right now, tonight or tomorrow. Pick one person in the next day or two and choose to be more transparent. Choose to be open in a situation where maybe you haven't been in the past. Do it with someone you already have a close relationship with, so it's not too scary. Choose a situation to create more transparency.

"Next, take an issue that you ordinarily wouldn't discuss with someone straight on. Maybe it's one of those undiscussable issues. Choose to bring it out for discussion, and see what the results are.

"These are two things you could do in any relationship right away, using your judgment as to how best to apply them. Here's a third: make a commitment and keep it. Make a commitment with another person and keep it, and make another one and keep it. You'll build trust with yourself because you make commitments and keep them, but you will also build trust with others. See, when you make a commitment, you build hope. When you keep a commitment, you build trust.

So making and keeping commitments is another immediate way to start to increase trust in a relationship.

What were the key lessons from this interview about living your passion?

1. Trust is the highest form of human motivation.

2. Distrust imposes a tax. High-trust relationships and organizations enjoy a dividend.

3. Trust always affects two measures: speed and cost. When trust goes down, things take longer and cost more. When trust goes up, things happen faster and at a lower cost.

4. As we seek to live our passions and fulfill our destiny, we are not isolated. Relationships are key to our ability to fulfill our personal destiny. Trust is fundamental to any relationship.

5. The process of building trust begins with yourself, with your own credibility, your own trustworthiness. It's hard to establish trust with others if you can't trust yourself.

6. There are two dimensions to building trust: character and competence. Both are vital to building trust.

7. When we extend trust, we give others the opportunity to prove themselves trustworthy.

8. Modeling trust by example comes first, then building trust in relationships, then teaching trust.

9. Building trust takes place over time, with increasing levels of trusting at each stage in a relationship.

10. When people feel trusted, it brings out the best in them.

11. It's important to seek to build trust with others. Just don't get ahead of yourself with extending too much trust beyond the other's character and/or competence.

12. Two ways anyone can increase trust in a relationship: create more transparency and take issues head-on.

13. Trust should be an explicit objective of every relationship and every organization.

Homework:

- Pick one person and choose to be more transparent with them;

- Select an issue you ordinarily wouldn't discuss head-on and choose to bring it out for discussion with someone you're close to; and

- Make a commitment with another person and keep it, then make another one and keep it.

THE BLISS IS
ALWAYS THERE

When people are deeply happy
they bring a sense of purpose with them
wherever they go, whatever circumstances they're in.
So if they're changing the oil in the car,
they bring a sense of joyful purpose even to that.

—*Marci Shimoff*

My name is Nicole McCance. I'm twenty-six years old, from Toronto. At eighteen I was living with my mother in a trailer, and my father had just passed away. I had no money, no support, and didn't know what direction to go.

But I had good grades. Over the next eight years, I completed college and graduate school, and became the youngest psychotherapist in Toronto. I quickly built a very successful private practice and have been fortunate to enjoy a great deal of personal and professional success, but something was still missing.

In the fall of 2006, Janet Attwood came to Toronto, and I took The Passion Test. As I wrote down my passions, all of the dreams and hopes of the past years came together in one sentence: "I am a famous transformational leader uplifting humanity." Just writing it down put a huge smile on my face. As I got clear on my top five, I realized how important "traveling the world" is to me, but I wasn't yet living it.

In that moment, I discovered that for all the success I've enjoyed, my soul's purpose was not yet fulfilled. While I love working with clients one on one, my desire is to make a profound difference in the world by inspiring hundreds of people at a time to wake up to their own greatness. The Passion Test showed me a whole new part of myself and Janet's presentation gave me the courage to follow my heart.

Janet kept telling us the how doesn't matter. She said your purpose unfolds naturally as long as you keep choosing in favor of your passions. I consciously set the intention that I would meet the right people to set my passions into action, having no idea how that would happen.

Nine days later, I attended a seminar. When I arrived, there were hundreds of people waiting in line to get into the seminar room. Two young men my age, named Kristian and Ali, were in line in front of me. We chatted then quickly scattered to take our seats in the large auditorium. I didn't think any more about the brief interaction.

The next day I ran into Kristian and Ali again. We talked some more and I got to know them a little better. At lunch time I was about to go to lunch with a new friend from the seminar when I had the feeling I should go back inside to see if there was anyone else who wanted to join us. I stood for a moment, not sure who I was looking for when I heard my name being called. It was Ali.

Inside I heard Janet's voice saying:

There are no mistakes in the universe.

It turns out that Kristian and Ali were in the process of finishing their studies to become chiropractors. Over salad, they told me about their cycling trip across Canada in the summer of 2005. They had visited Boys and Girls Clubs, spreading a message of wellness.

They told me about their dream of putting on events inspiring hundreds of youths while cycling from Los Angeles to New York City, in the summer of 2007. They were looking for three people to join them and were animated as they shared their vision of uplifting humanity while going on a ten-week cycling adventure across the country.

As I listened, I got more and more excited. Here were my two top passions being handed to me by two strangers.

"Can I come?" fell out of my mouth. At the same time, my ego was screaming that I hadn't been on a bicycle since pink streamers were in style and I had a private practice to run, but every inch of my being was saying *yes*! As all these thoughts ran through my head, I remembered Janet's instruction:

**Whenever you are faced with a choice, a decision, or
an opportunity, choose in favor of your passions.**

That day I chose to follow my passions. Ali and Kristian were thrilled at my excitement, but the new tour team still needed two more cyclists to make the tour happen.

The next day I invited my new friends to a party inspired by Jack Canfield, called Come as you'll be in 2011. I brought my friend Christy. Ali and Kristian brought a friend named Shah. Magic happened that night.

We each showed up, in character, as who we would be in five years. We talked about our passions and dreams. It wasn't long before we all knew. This was our cycling team. We called ourselves The Dream Team, with the intention of making our own and others' dreams come true.

I told my new friends about The Passion Test and the profound effect it had on me. They all did The Passion Test and loved it. We shared a passion for uplifting the world, and we set our Markers to attract all the help we needed to make our dream come true.

We met morning and night, making our plans. Then early one morning a thought popped into my head, "Why don't we take The Passion Test on tour and have youth across America become clear on their purpose and destiny?"

I talked with my team and they loved the idea. Someone I know had made arrangements to have Janet speak to a large group in Toronto, so I was able to get Janet's phone number from her. I called and asked if the five of us could have dinner with her when she came to town. We had something *really* exciting to tell her about.

When the day arrived, we could hardly wait. We told Janet our idea and her immediate reaction was, "Of course! And I think we can plus it even more." The next morning, Janet connected us with Colleen Adams, director of events at Perry Ellis and we were on our way.

Our team put our heads together and named the cycling tour Unleash America. After talking with Janet, she suggested we add the word *passion,* and we all agreed. "Unleash America's Passion" was born! As we have applied The Passion Test principles, each of us has gone deep inside and discovered things about ourselves we never fully came to grips with before.

We found out that each of us has had some incredibly traumatic experiences. As we talked we realized that these experiences allow us to connect with kids and show them what's possible in ways we could never have done otherwise. Through this it's become clear to us that every moment really is a gift, and the gift shows up just when it's needed.

As things have unfolded, we have gotten so much support. Colleen Adams added her own passion for transforming the lives of youth in detention centers. As we cycle across the United States taking kids through The Passion Test at Boys and Girls Clubs, Janet and Colleen will join us in five of the cities to deliver The Passion Test to youth detention centers.

Our tour is now being sponsored by the Learning Forum Foundation, a nonprofit educational organization created by Bobbi DePorter, cofounder of the famous SuperCamp program. Jay Abraham, one of the top marketers in the world, is helping us with the planning. Marci Shimoff and Lisa Nichols, both stars of *The Secret* and bestselling authors in the Chicken Soup for the Soul series, have joined our board. Dr. Ted Morter of Morter Health Systems is also helping us. In addition, we are receiving incredible support from people all across the United States.

Our story is not finished, yet just the process of creating and planning it has transformed us. The five of us have become so close. There is a mutual caring and support between us, which I treasure. And the power of a shared vision has completely energized our lives. I can't wait to see how it all turns out, and, already, thanks to The Passion Test, I know what it means to live a passionate, turned-on life.

Enjoying the Trip

Marci Shimoff has been a #1 *New York Times* bestselling author multiple times. Her latest book, *Happy for No Reason*, provides deep insights into that most elusive yet desired experience, happiness. We sat with Marci and asked her about what it takes to be happy, and we'll share that with you soon, but first let's talk about your own experience of happiness.

What is it that creates real happiness? When have you experienced happiness in your life? Many people associate happiness with achievement. "I will be happy when I get a promotion, make more money, find my soul mate."

Have you ever known anyone who is completely goal oriented and has achieved much in their life but doesn't seem very happy? Unfortunately, it happens all too often.

Think about the biggest goal you ever set and achieved sometime in the past. How long did you spend working to achieve that goal? How long did the celebration of its achievement last? Once you had achieved the goal, did it make you happy?

The key to happiness is to discover it in every moment, not to wait for it to arrive with the achievement of some future goal. Living a passionate life is the fulfillment that comes from the process of creation. The happiness that comes from achieving a goal is fleeting at best. Remember what Debbie Ford shared when she talked about her experience of becoming a #1 *New York Times* bestselling author?

Happiness is a fickle beast. It has a tendency to come and go as we feel expanded and contracted. According to Marci, "being happy for no reason" means experiencing a state of

deep inner fulfillment that comes from a profound connection with your own nature.

In one of the ancient Vedic texts from India there is this
saying:

"You have control over action alone, never over its fruits."

You have no way of insuring that you will achieve any goal
in your life (the fruit of your action). The only thing you can
determine is what you do, what action you take, to create the
life you choose to live.

This is why it's so important that you love what you do.
Most of your life is about the process of creating, not the outcomes or results of that process. Once you've realized a dream
or a goal, you'll celebrate it, enjoy it, and then you will be back
in the process of creating your next dream.

Happiness arises spontaneously when you love the process.
Remember when we talked about the difference between passions and goals in part 1? Passions are about how you live your
life. Goals are about what you choose to create in your life.

That's why, when we asked you to make the list of the
things you love, we asked you to complete the sentence, "When
my life is ideal I am _____."

Completing that sentence helps you define your process. It
helps you define what elements you need to live with passion
and purpose. It helps you define what you need to be happy in
the process.

If you write, "living in a beautiful home overlooking the
ocean," your passion is the "living" part of that sentence. Living is a process. Your goal may be to acquire a beautiful home
overlooking the ocean, but if you acquire it and never live in
it, are you living your passion?

So how do you live this passion if you don't yet have the

home? Whenever you are faced with a choice, a decision, or an opportunity, you ask yourself, "Will this bring me closer to living in my beautiful home, or will it take me farther away?" If the answer is that it will, then you go for it. If not, then you decline.

As you make these decisions, you will find yourself fueled by the remarkable process of the unfolding of your destiny. There will almost certainly be challenges, just as the Unleash America's Passion team discovered, and within those challenges the greatest gifts are buried.

This Highway Is on Solid Ground

Hiding beneath the layers of beliefs, concepts, and ideas that have led to your current life situation is a wonderful world. It's a world of joy, of bliss, of fullness. Like the sun, which is always there behind the clouds, the experience of that blissful world is never completely gone, it's just out of sight.

Janet learned about this world years ago. It's taken some surprising experiences to discover how to part the clouds.

> Many years before Chris and I were married, I had taken a course on deep breathing in Sweden. The instructor explained that this kind of breathing can sometimes be very painful when you are in the middle of the process. She then told us, "Whenever this happens, go into the pain completely and eventually you will transcend it."
>
> I never forgot those words.
>
> "Go into the pain completely and eventually you will transcend it."
>
> There were times when Chris and I were married that

things came up for one or both of us that were very painful. Chris's initial reaction in those days would be to shut down completely, and he'd want to run away (sound familiar?). When this happened, I explained what I had learned about "going into the pain."

"Separation is painful," I would tell him. "When you shut down you are actually burying the pain, and inevitably it will come up again. Instead, go into the pain. On the other side of the pain is peace, bliss."

At first these words were met with total resistance.

Then one day Chris came home from work completely traumatized. He had been doing everything he could to save his company. Despite all of his best efforts, his partner, the company's founder, kept making the same wrong decisions. He didn't listen to Chris's advice, and the company was on the verge of losing everything.

The day Chris discovered there was no money to make payroll, he was devastated. When he came home from work I could see that the pressure of trying to save the company from its fate had finally taken its toll on him.

We went to bed that night and at about 3:00 a.m., Chris woke me up. He was shaking uncontrollably, and it wouldn't stop.

"Go into the pain, Chris," I told him.

"Lie down, breathe in and out deeply, and go completely into the pain," I pleaded.

Unable to catch his breath, and not knowing what else to do, Chris lay down on the bed and followed my instructions.

"Chris, give in to the pain 100 percent," I said. "Don't resist."

After about sixty minutes of continuous breathing

and letting go completely into the pain he was experiencing, Chris looked up at me with the most peaceful smile.

It was in that moment he understood, as I had, that on the other side of the pain, physical, mental, or emotional, is peace, silence, bliss.

I had reason to remember this in a completely different way, many years later.

I was holding a large pot of boiling water when all of a sudden I lost my balance and the water, starting at my neck, splashed all down the front of me.

Just remembering that moment still makes me wince. It was one of the most physically painful experiences I have ever had.

Within a matter of seconds, I had severe burns all over the front of my body. After being treated for the burns, the only way I could be comfortable was to lie completely still on my back in bed. Any movement would send me screaming at the top of my lungs. I couldn't have any sheets or covers touching me since even the slightest graze from the sheet would send me writhing in agony.

I remember lying in bed for hours, totally consumed by the pain, thinking, "Will this nightmare torture ever stop?" No matter how I positioned my body, nothing gave me the slightest amount of comfort. The pain was completely exhausting.

Then something remarkable happened. Unable to stand the pain any longer, I remembered the words my instructor from Sweden had shared with me so many years back, "Go into the pain."

As I lay there in bed, consumed by the intense pain, I focused all of my attention 100 percent on the pain, just

> as my instructor had told me to do and just as I had ad-
> vised Chris many years back.
>
> At first it was the most agonizing experience, and
> then as if by magic my consciousness pierced through
> the horrific wall of pain to a painless state. Once I sur-
> rendered to the pain totally, I no longer felt any pain
> whatsoever, and instead I felt total peace. Total 100 per-
> cent painless peace.
>
> "Go into the pain completely and eventually you will
> transcend it," my instructor had said.
>
> And then I did, and I found once again, "The bliss is
> always there!"

This bliss is the same state Marci calls "happy for no reason."
It's always there. It's always available. But when you've been
hanging on to beliefs, concepts, and ideas that argue with reality, they keep you separated from that state.

Mental or emotional pain is the result of attachment to
false concepts. As long as you hang on to what you believe is
true, in contradiction to reality, you will experience pain.
When you run away from the pain or dull it with alcohol,
food, drugs, TV, or any other escape, you only bury it. It will
come back again, guaranteed.

When you allow yourself to feel the pain, as uncomfortable
as it may be at first, you begin the process of healing. Some people call this "standing in the fire." When you can stand in it and
feel it completely, there will come a point when you discover
the bliss, and you will find yourself "happy for no reason."

Marci Shimoff has written a whole book on this topic. Let's
hear what she has to say about happiness, passion, and purpose.

Marci Shimoff

Marci Shimoff is the one of the women's faces behind the biggest self-help book phenomenon in history, Chicken Soup for the Soul. *Her six bestselling titles in the series have met with stunning success, selling more than 13 million copies worldwide in thirty-three languages. They have been on the* New York Times *bestseller list for a total of 108 weeks (number one for 12 weeks) and have also topped the* USA Today *and* Publishers Weekly *lists. Marci is one of the bestselling female nonfiction authors of all time, and she is one of the stars of the bestselling book and movie phenomenon* The Secret.

Her latest book is appropriately called Happy for No Reason.

"We all come from the same source, and that source is pure joy, pure love, and pure happiness. It's our essential nature. In order to experience true happiness we just need to feel that connection to our source. When people are living a life aligned with their passions then they're living a life aligned with their soul and their soul's destiny—and that is what brings us happiness.

"I have spent a number of years following great leaders, teachers, and wise people who emanate a state of happiness that seems deeply grounded, and they carry it with them wherever they go. You could put them in really bad circumstances and they would still be happy.

"I thought, 'That's the kind of happiness I want.' People in our society are so busy trying to acquire things in order to make themselves happy, but it never really works. Once you reach one of your goals there's another goal around the corner, and it's always out in the future—it's a temporary happiness.

"I know there is a state called 'happy for no reason.' It's a neurophysiological state of peace and well-being. We have all kinds of physiological equipment that can measure this kind of state, and experiencing it is possible. It's a state that's not dependent on circumstances.

"There's an old saying that success leaves clues, and if you study the behaviors of successful people and follow these behaviors, you too will be successful. The same is true with happiness. Happiness leaves clues. All you have to do is look at a group of truly happy people and you will see there are key characteristics that are similar.

"Probably the first and most important of these is an overall feeling of trust in the universe. Einstein once said that the most important question you can ever ask is, 'Is this a friendly universe?'

"In other words, is there benevolence in the universe, and is the universe out to support you? What I've found with truly happy people is they all feel a sense of trust that the universe and life are unfolding exactly as they should. Even though the outer circumstances may not always look the way they want them to look—because we can't control the world around us—they are still happy.

"In addition, truly happy people look for the gift in anything that happens. So if something doesn't exactly match what they want, they're able to see the gift in it. They're able to expect what is. They also lean into or favor what it is that makes them feel good. Rather than putting all their attention and energy into what makes them feel bad, they habituate or favor what makes them feel good.

"When people are deeply happy they bring a sense of purpose with them wherever they go, whatever circumstances they're in. So if they're changing the oil in the car, they bring a sense of joyful purpose even to that.

"The statistics on people retiring are quite profound. When people retire they very often die. And why do they die? They die because they've lost their sense of purpose in life. Our purpose helps bring us our joy.

"I love to tell this story—the happiest person I've known in my life was my father. My father loved what he did. He was a dentist, and he loved being a dentist. He retired at age seventy-two, reluctantly, and he knew the statistics about what happens to people when they retire.

"So he said, 'Well, I better find myself something else to do, some other purpose, something else I love.' He analyzed what he loved about dentistry and realized it wasn't about putting fillings in people's mouths. He loved working in intricate ways with his hands, in ways that he felt were artistic.

"So at age seventy-two he took up needlepoint, and he became a master needlepointer. He loved doing needlepoint! I remember when he was about eighty-five I went home one day to visit and he had just begun the biggest and most intricate needlepoint I have ever seen. Here's an eighty-five-year-old man beginning this huge project.

"I said to him, 'Dad, how long is this going to take you to finish?' And he said, "Honey, I figure at the pace I'm going it's going to take me about four years." An eighty-five-year-old man beginning a four-year project—but he had a sense of purpose. And did he complete that project? You bet he did!

"He completed it, and I think it was that feeling of being present in the moment, bringing his love and his purpose, his passion, to what he was doing that enabled him to make exquisite needlepoint. He actually has won needlepoint awards throughout all of California.

"Feeling a sense of purpose in whatever we're doing, at all times, no matter what age, is so critical to our happiness. And being happy allows us to bring joy to whatever it is we're doing.

"My favorite way to develop a sense of purpose is to take The Passion Test. And that's what I tell everybody to do to help them get aligned with their purpose. In addition to that, you can start noticing what in your life makes your soul sing.

"Most people are so busy going through the motions of the day that they don't pay attention to what their heart and soul are saying to them. That's really the magic formula for knowing what your passions are. What is it that makes your heart expand? What makes you feel full? What really makes your soul sing?

"Then watch the signs the universe brings to you. Because there are always synchronicities and signs that can guide you along the way and help you see the way to being more aligned with your passions.

"The most important thing is to listen to your heart, to listen to the source of your inner wisdom and your inner knowingness, rather than listening to your mind. The mind tells you what you should be doing, what you think you have to be doing, what you need to be doing, what everybody else expects you to be doing. But the heart, if you listen deeply enough, tells you what your soul is saying. When you live from that place you will be happy for no reason and living your passions.

"Love is the most powerful force in the universe. Nothing is more powerful than love. When you let love guide your answers, let love guide your purpose, and let love guide your life, it can only be a life of pure happiness, pure truth, and pure joy."

What were the key lessons from this interview about living your passion?

1. We all come from the same source, and that source is pure joy, pure love, and pure happiness.
2. When you are living life aligned with your passions you're living life aligned with your soul and your soul's destiny. That is what brings happiness.
3. There is a state called "happy for no reason." It's a neurophysiological state of peace and well-being.
4. Happiness leaves clues. Truly happy people have key characteristics that are similar.
5. Truly happy people feel a sense of trust that the universe and life are unfolding exactly as they should.
6. Truly happy people look for the gift in anything that happens.
7. When people are deeply happy they bring a sense of purpose with them wherever they go, whatever circumstances they're in.
8. There is a magic formula for knowing what your passions are: What is it that makes your heart expand? What makes you feel full? What really makes your soul sing?

9. The most important thing is to listen to your heart. Listen to the source of your inner wisdom and your inner knowingness, rather than to your mind.

10. When you let love guide your life, it can only be a life of pure happiness, pure truth, and pure joy.

UNITED AT OUR CORE

> You are not here merely to make a living. You are
> here in order to enable the world to live more
> amply, with greater vision, with a finer spirit of
> hope and achievement. You are here to enrich the
> world, and you impoverish yourself if you forget
> the errand.
>
> —*Woodrow Wilson*

My name is Nicole Wild. As executive director of the Women's Alliance, a national charity dedicated to empowering low-income women, I have been living my passion to help women in need for the last ten years.

In January 2006, I was a new mum and working to open our resale store, called Chapter 2, in a very tough neighborhood of Miami.

Linda Peterson is co-owner of Peterson's Harley-Davidson. She and I have been working together on and off for more than ten years. We're both fully committed in our quest to transform the lives of women in transition from homelessness to a new life. We share the desire to honor our mothers who sacrificed themselves with the hope that we, their daughters, will find our true voices and destinies.

In January, Linda called and let me know that she was going to sponsor a Black Tie and Blues Jeans Gala honoring her husband on April 21. She wanted the Women's Alliance to be the charitable recipient of the event. I was thrilled.

Linda and I worked hand in hand preparing for the event, going to women's meetings and get-togethers throughout the city. At one particular meeting we met the CEO of a major magazine. She congratulated us for our work and out of our mouths popped, "Well, that's the power behind the passion."

She replied, "That is the best slogan I've ever heard. Be sure to get the domain name. It's fabulous!"

Linda went straight home and Googled "Powerbehind-thepassion.com." Near the top of the list was The Passion Test. Intrigued, she went to the website and before I knew it had ordered the e-book, purchased two softcover copies, and taken the Test.

Linda loved the simple process. She was amazed at how it helped her clarify what is most important to her. She also saw how it could help our homeless women get a new start. She immediately wanted Janet as the speaker at our annual luncheon, planned this year for two hundred homeless women in Miami.

Linda showed up at Chapter 2 like a force of nature and stood with conviction at my desk, asking that we e-mail Chris and Janet with an appeal for two hundred signed copies of the book and a conference call. Within twenty-four hours after sending the e-mail with a prayer, Janet responded: "Let's talk."

During that first call, Janet let us know she holds a special passion for women in need. Her mother, she explained, had struggled her entire life with similar problems. We invited Janet to come to Miami to present The Passion Test to our group of two hundred homeless women. There wasn't a moment's hesitation. "Yes!" she said immediately, and then, "Let me check my calendar."

The Black Tie and Blue Jeans Gala was a huge success, and we knew we still needed a third person for our Power Behind the Passion team, someone to provide balance and give our team a unique perspective.

Around that time, I reconnected with Thomas Cook, a dynamo at creating strategic alliances and networking. In the past, I had worked closely with Thomas on special initiatives for the Women's Alliance that included celebrity outreach to Oprah Winfrey, the Duchess of York, Ellen DeGeneres, and Rosie O'Donnell, to name a few.

Like Linda and me, Thomas was on a mission. His experience of physically dying (twice!) and surviving led to the emergence of a man committed to helping others.

In June, 2006, Thomas, Linda, and I met in Washington DC, and our Power Behind the Passion team was formed. We committed ourselves to proving that it doesn't matter where you come from. We are all united at the deepest level. Every one of us can reach inside and make a difference in the lives of others. Yet we still didn't know exactly what direction our project would take us.

On July 31, my daughter, Isabella, woke me up at 5:00 a.m. As I sat putting her back to sleep, I was sparked by the idea of the "red paper clip blog phenomenon" (the fellow who traded a red paper clip for a house). The Passion Test had ignited our imaginations and I thought, "Why not up-trade a copy of The Passion Test into a multimillion-dollar donation for the Women's Alliance?" This would be our first Power Behind the Passion project.

Within a month after posting the book on Craigslist, Dr. Donna Goldstein of Hollywood, Florida, had traded a $175 piece of art for the book. Then Mark Victor Hansen, co-creator of the Chicken Soup for the Soul series, traded $875 worth of his products for the artwork.

Next, entrepreneur/philanthropist Jim Kelley traded all the parts with matching serial numbers for a 1999 Harley-Davidson motorcycle. Then Drew Peterson, Linda's husband and co-owner of Peterson's Harley-Davidson of Miami, stepped in. Drew provided a 2007 Harley engine and transmission. Now we had everything we needed to build a bike worthy of its mission.

Our team organized a Passion Run to raise awareness for our project. On March 31, 2007, we lured an elite group of one hundred Harley-Davidson riders, supporters, and believers for the event. With an escort of sixteen policemen leading the way, we proudly rode through the city of Miami, waving to passersby and smiling from ear to ear.

Jim Kelley flew in from Boston and during the event made a deal with Drew Peterson to copartner and build the Tigertail Motorcycle (the name of our exclusive bike) for the Power Behind the Passion project. Janet rode in the police escorted event as a special guest. Once again she got to witness the true spirit of The Passion Test in action.

We've come to realize that anything is possible. You just have to be clear on what you want to show up in your life.

The Passion Test opened the door for us and it doesn't seem to stop.

Janet's talk at our "Butterflies for Hope" luncheon for the two hundred homeless women in transition was an overwhelming success. As a result, Janet, in conjunction with the Women's Alliance, has now created a CD package titled *The Empowered Women's Series* that is played at homeless shelters in Miami every month. This life-changing series features Byron Katie, Lynne Twist, Marci Shimoff, Lisa Nichols, Rickie Byars Beckwith, and other well-known transformational women leaders.

We're on fire now, and this is just the beginning. The Power Behind the Passion team is preparing to launch the You're One in a Million nationwide campaign to sell a million raffle tickets at a dollar each for the Tigertail bike drawing. We intend to prove what The Passion Test has shown us: that all things are possible—honoring mothers and caretakers everywhere and the important work of the Women's Alliance.

It is the thought that you are separate from the world and people around you that gives rise to fear and suffering. When you realize that this sense of separation is, in fact, a false concept, a new world of possibilities opens up, as Nicole, Linda, and Thomas have discovered. Take a look at the miracles the Power the Behind the Passion team is creating as they help bring our world together, by going to

www.thepassiontest.com/powerbehindthepassion.com.

Then start thinking about the miracles you can begin creating in your own life.

Traveling the Cosmic Highway

Your passions are like bread crumbs, leading you to discover who you really are. You can take The Passion Test as often as you find it useful, even every few days or weeks as you follow those bread crumbs. At the very least, take it every six months. Like peeling the layers of an onion, each time you will discover more about yourself.

When you identify what you love most, care about most, what matters most to you, right now in this moment, you learn something about yourself. Then as you live your life with the intention of choosing in favor of those passions, you learn more about yourself, just as the Unleash America's Passion team did.

Sometimes it will be easy to choose for your passions. Sometimes it will be more difficult. Sometimes your passions will change quickly and dramatically, just as Janet's did when she found out her stepmother was terminally ill.

In every case, you will learn more about who you really are. We encourage you to take The Passion Test at least every six months because it will help you assess the knowledge you are gaining about yourself.

Whether it's six months or six weeks, if you discover that you simply are unable to choose in favor of the five passions you have written down, this is a signal that it's time to take the Test again. Why? Because there is something that is more important to you than what you have written down and you are favoring that.

Sometimes the mind will fool you. You'll write something down, and you might sincerely believe that it is most important to you. But your actions will tell the real story.

So if you find yourself choosing in favor of something other than what you have written down, notice. Then go back and take the Test again, paying attention to what it is you are choosing. Whatever you are choosing, that is what is really important to you, at least right now.

If your choices are not matching what you believe you care about, use The Work of Byron Katie, or any other tool you find that works, to investigate the beliefs, concepts, and ideas that are leading to your choices.

When you choose in favor of things other than what is really important to you, you are making those choices because you are holding on to some false belief, false concept, or false idea. Investigate what is really true for you, and then begin choosing in favor of your passions.

Now some people might say, isn't always choosing in favor of what you want awfully selfish? What about what other people want or need?

We always say, "When you do what's best for you, what brings you the greatest joy, then everyone wins!" Think about it.

Most of us have grown up with beliefs about what is "good" and what is "bad." These beliefs are what we mean by the difference between "your will" and "God's will," or if you prefer, "life's will." As long as you hold on to what you believe is "good" even when it doesn't feel good, you are saying, "I know better how to organize the universe." This is what Debbie Ford was talking about when she advised us to "resign as general manager of the universe."

Not too long ago Janet was giving a seminar when a woman raised her hand and said:

"How can I choose in favor of my passions when I have my children at home?"

Janet asked her, "What is your passion?"

She replied, "I really want to begin working around fashion."

Janet then asked, "Are you ever frustrated at home when you are thinking you can't live your passions?"

The woman replied, "Yes, all the time."

Next Janet asked, "Do you ever get angry with your kids or your husband because of feeling so trapped and frustrated?"

"I do."

"So tell me. What's best: Possibly finding a great part-time job working in the fashion industry and then spending time with your kids, or keeping things the way they are? What message are you giving your kids by not doing what makes you happy?

"Can you be open enough to consider that maybe the reason you have this desire is because you are supposed to fulfill it?

"And can you see how this might create happiness inside of you, end the frustration, and create a more loving family life?"

Right in that moment, the light went on. This woman could see that she might be able to live her passions and care for her children at the same time.

You don't have to know the how. You just need to get clear on the what.

For most mothers, their children and family are among their top passions. But when a mother finds herself yearning for something else, there is a reason. As long as you strain and struggle to do the "selfless" thing, as this woman was doing, you will make yourself miserable, feel victimized and unhappy, all in the name of being of service to those you love. What's wrong with this picture?

When you are happy and fulfilled in your own life then your cup is full and it becomes easy and natural to give to others.

All we are asking is that you stay open, clarify what it is you choose to create in your life, and keep your attention on those things. Let the universe organize the how.

Life is here for our joy. Following the path of what you love means letting go of your concepts of what is best and trusting that you are being led to what is best, not only for you, but for everyone else at the same time.

Where the Cosmic Highway Is Taking Us

As you come to know yourself more deeply, your passions will change less and less over time. You'll discover your passions can be expressed through a variety of channels that all describe the way you choose to live your life.

Why would your passions change less often? Because the more deeply you dive into any aspect of life, you connect with increasingly universal principles that are more stable and unchanging. The surface of life is always changing. The depth of life changes little, if at all.

In their book, *Success Built to Last*, our friends Stewart Emery, Mark Thompson, and Jerry Porras investigated what leads to enduring success. Enduring success tells us that the people who have experienced it have learned something that expresses some fundamental principles all of us can apply in our own lives.

These authors interviewed over three hundred people who had enjoyed success in their chosen fields for twenty years or more. They included Michael Dell, Bill Gates, Jimmy Carter, Maya Angelou, Sir Richard Branson, and many others.

The common characteristic of these people is that they had all developed the habit of choosing in favor of those things that have the deepest meaning for them. In our words, they developed the habit of choosing in favor of their passions.

Discovering what gives meaning to your life and identifying your core passions is a process. The Passion Test is a useful tool in that process, and as you identify your core passions, you will find those things tend to change very little.

When Marci Shimoff's father found himself faced with retirement, he made a choice to continue doing what he loved. But he could no longer do it in the way he had for many years. So he was forced to go deeper. While dentistry had been the way he expressed his passion for his entire adult life, when he examined what he loved about dentistry he discovered it was the ability to do fine, highly skilled work with his hands.

Marci's father was creative enough to realize he could express that same passion in an entirely different way by taking up needlepoint. Fortunately, he didn't have the false belief that needlepoint is only for women. As a result, he lived out the last twenty years of his long life, happy, fulfilled, and continuing to do what he loved, in an entirely new way.

The great thing about The Passion Test is that there is no way you can fail it. We encourage you to simply take the Test and not worry much about how deep or profound your passions are. Don't worry much about whether you have discovered your "core" passions. Just take the Test regularly and choose in favor of your passions. Your core passions will begin to emerge naturally.

We're All on the Same Highway

Today physicists tell us that at the deepest level of Nature the differences we perceive with our senses cease to exist. At that deepest level, there is one, unified, unchanging field of life, from which all the diversity and change we perceive arises.

There are quantum physicists today who make the case that this unified field at the basis of the physical world is, in fact, a field of consciousness. It has the ability to know itself. And it is in the process of knowing itself through each of our individual lives. We are the expressions of that fundamental consciousness coming to know our own true nature. The closer you come to that true nature, the more joy you experience.

Discovering your unique gifts, your special talents, your deeply felt passions leads you to deeper and deeper realizations that in turn bring more and more fulfillment. Soon you will discover that this is the whole purpose of life—to experience ever-expanding joy. That's why we say, "What you love and God's will for you are one and the same." God's will is for you to experience more and more delight in your life.

This is true whether you believe in God or not. The structure of the laws of Nature work in just this way, bringing you more and more delight the more aligned you are with what you love.

Nature's Guidance System is hardwired into the structure of existence. When you listen to those messages, taking action when you feel expanded and stopping, taking a break, and reflecting when you feel contracted, you will discover your life moving toward greater and greater fulfillment.

Because of the ultimate connectedness of all life, the more deeply you connect with your passions, the more joy you will discover comes from giving and serving others. In serving others, you are really serving yourself.

First you will discover how unique and special you are. You will uncover the things that make you uniquely suited to give your gifts. You will realize there is no one else who can do you as well as you can. And there is no one who can serve the world or the people around you the way you are able to.

Then as this realization becomes clearer and clearer, you will discover the profound joy that comes from giving your gifts. And you will be surprised at how your world seems to almost magically organize to allow you to give your gifts in ways you cannot even imagine right now.

Having said all this, don't think the process of discovery will be all peaches and cream. Learning to trust in the benevolence of the universe, that everything is being organized perfectly for you, is a big step. Getting to the point of having the confidence to follow your own inner guidance doesn't necessarily come easily.

Here's a taste of how Janet has experienced it as she has gotten more deeply in touch with her own true nature:

> I had just gotten my ego destroyed, mutilated, and pulverized while in the presence of a well-known guru in Puttaparthi, India. On my way back to the United States from my less than cosmic experience, deflated and depressed and unable to sleep, I pulled out my jewelry supplies and started making jewelry on the plane (this was before 9/11).
>
> I had become quite adept at making beautiful pearl

bracelets, earrings, and necklaces and found through my travels that airline stewardesses made great customers. I could easily sell two hundred to four hundred dollars worth of jewelry to them on the flight. The stewardesses loved that I offered them special "up-in-the-air discounts" and had a blast walking back and forth from their mirror to my seat, buying two to three pieces of jewelry at a time.

As I was creating a pearl bracelet on the Bangalore to Amsterdam leg, a rather large Indian woman passed by my seat. Seeing all of the beads on my lap she said to me, "What are you doing?"

"Making jewelry," I replied.

"Nice," she said.

"What are you doing?" I asked.

"I am on my way to speak to the United Nations about the repression of women in India."

"Cool!"

Enthralled by her mission, I asked if she would like to sit with me. Interestingly, I had moved my seat when I first got on the plane. I later discovered that had I stayed in my assigned seat, this same woman would have been right next to me. Some things are just meant to be.

"Want to learn how to make a bracelet?" I asked.

"Why not?" she replied and sat down.

"My name is Janet."

"Hi, Janet. My name is Ruth."

While teaching Ruth how to make bracelets for her two daughters, she explained that she ran an organization of over 26,000 women in Bangalore, India. Ruth told me that her organization was created for the sole purpose of supporting women who had been repressed.

"Repression of women in India is rampant. The men

beat them, rape them, marry them for their dowries, and then abandon them," she said.

After three hours of talking and beading, Ruth had made two really awful bracelets for her daughters, all the while talking nonstop about the women's organization she ran.

By the time we arrived in Amsterdam, we had bonded completely.

As we were saying our good-byes and exchanging e-mail addresses, Ruth said to me, "Janet, could poor women learn the art of jewelry making and make money like you do with it?"

"Why not?" I replied.

Happy to hear my answer, Ruth then turned to me with a serious look on her face and asked, "Would you consider coming back to India to teach poor girls jewelry making someday?"

"Absolutely, I would be honored!"

And with that, Ruth and I hugged and promised we would keep in touch.

When I returned to the United States I still had two weeks of vacation left and no plans. It was one and a half weeks before Christmas, and for some odd reason I didn't have any Christmas spirit in me at all.

Every day I was home I couldn't think of anything but Ruth and her request. After my fourth day home, Ruth and her girls had become my one and only thought.

On my fifth day back from India, still completely consumed with thoughts of Ruth and teaching the girls in her organization how to make jewelry, I went online and purchased a ticket back to India.

On my sixth day back, I packed all of my jewelry supplies along with a small suitcase of clothes and flew back to India.

It wasn't until I was on the plane from Cedar Rapids to Minneapolis that it began to hit me. I was going back to India and I hadn't even received a reply to my e-mail to Ruth telling her I was coming. I started to melt down.

A chill of panic raced through my body. Here it was Christmas time and I was on my way back to India, where I didn't have any real friends, and I was traveling by myself. I'd have no presents to open and no one to share Christmas Day with. I felt completely vulnerable and alone.

Overwhelmed by my own impulsive nature, I started crying uncontrollably. By the time I reached Minneapolis I was sure I had to be the most ridiculously eccentric person on the planet. Mortified and deeply depressed, I beelined straight for a phone to call my good friend Radhika, who was among a small handful of people I had shared my impending adventure with.

"Radhika, what was I thinking? What's wrong with me? Have I gone completely crazy? I haven't even heard from Ruth yet and here I am on my way back to India. What was I thinking?"

I continued ranting on as Radhika just listened on the other end.

"And that's not all; the worst part of my lunacy is that I paid top dollar for this ticket. Geez, Ruth could be in America for all I know."

Aware that I had been going on nonstop for over ten minutes, I apologized to Radhika and said, "I called because I wanted to tell you I'm not going to India. I'm coming back to Iowa and I need a ride from the airport. Any chance you can come pick me up?"

In a slow, even, measured voice, Radhika said to me, "Jani, get on the plane. The force is with you. Get on the plane, everything will work out. I just know it."

"Are you sure?" I wailed, terrified at the prospect of making the wrong choice.

"One hundred percent," she said.

"Okay, but I sure hope you're right."

With more than a little trepidation, I said good-bye to Radhika and boarded the plane.

When I landed in Amsterdam I ran to the business center and, with trembling hands, checked to see if Ruth had replied to my e-mail.

As I prayed for a miracle, Ruth's e-mail magically popped up.

"Wonderful," it read. "I will pick you up at the airport and will have twenty homeless girls ready for you to teach jewelry making the next day. God bless you, Jani. Love, Ruth."

True to her word, Ruth had twenty girls waiting for me when I arrived with all of my jewelry supplies. Sitting on a dirty floor in the stifling heat, I taught the girls how to make jewelry all week. My biggest challenge was that I didn't speak Hindi and they didn't speak English. The two translators Ruth had presented me with didn't really speak English either. I soon learned that make-believe sign language was universal and although things went slowly, all of us actually started to understand one another.

As the days wore on, I noticed that the girls had on the same tattered clothes every day.

"They don't own more than what is on their backs, Janet. Worst of all, they live in cardboard shanties by the side of the road," Ruth said. "In the summer they sleep near the highways instead of inside their cardboard boxes because the sound of the cars scares the rats away. If they stay in their shanties, the rats gnaw at their feet when they are asleep."

Ruth told me more horror stories about how their fathers raped them and how their parents made them beg for rupees in the sweltering sun for ten to thirteen hours at a time.

To say the least, I was humbled by these little girls, their indomitable spirits, and their undying courage.

As I looked around the room, each one of the girls was beading away, smiling and laughing while they made their jewelry pieces. I knew this had to be one of the greatest highlights of their lives to date.

Finally, when our week was over, each and every one of the girls had mastered the art of jewelry making. I was so impressed with their talents that I graduated each one of them into my newly formed Janima Jewelry Club.

As each of the girls lined up to give me a hug goodbye, I started sobbing. For this special moment, Ruth had taught them a few words of English.

"Thank you, Janima," they said, with tears in their eyes.

"We love you, Janima. We love you," they all chimed.

Looking into their beautiful, innocent eyes, I was filled with emotion. Crying nonstop, I took each one of the girls into my arms and held her close to my heart. "Don't give up," I whispered into their ears. "And don't forget that I love you," I said.

Even though they didn't understand all of my words, there wasn't a dry eye to be found. Somehow in that week we had all transcended the boundary of speech and had adopted the universal language of the heart.

It was in that moment that I realized I was the one who had received the most. Every smile, every glance, every moment with each of the girls had been a gift to me from God. I knew my heart couldn't have gotten any bigger. It was exploding in huge, gigantic waves of thankfulness for this incredible opportunity to serve.

Flooded with emotion, I gave each one of them one big, long hug before turning on my heels and walking away.

As I was walking, I was aware of a deep sense of inner peace inside that had never been there before. And as I continued I heard Radhika's words echoing inside, "The force is with you."

The force *is* with you. Both the challenges and achievements of your life are there to support you in knowing yourself. They are guiding you to fulfill your purpose and live the fulfilling life you are meant to live.

Under the guidance of Ruth's daughter, the Janima Jewelry Club continued to provide support for these girls over the next two years, allowing them to make jewelry and earn money from sales of their jewelry in the United States.

Our final interview is with one of the foremost quantum physicists in the world today. It is physics that has finally shown us that we are truly united at our core. Today quantum physics has demonstrated that the diversity and apparent solidity of our physical world is an illusion. At more fundamental levels, beyond the molecular and atomic structures of physical matter, energy and matter become unified.

With this understanding it becomes more obvious why we feel increasing joy as we discover what unites us, because we are uncovering deeper levels of truth.

Dr. John Hagelin

Dr. John Hagelin is a world authority in the area of unified quantum field theories. His scientific contributions in the fields of particle physics and cosmology include some of the most cited references in the physical sciences. He is codeveloper of what is now considered the leading contender for a grand unified field theory, known as Supersymmetric Flipped SU(5).

Dr. Hagelin is unique among particle theorists in his dedicated efforts to apply the latest scientific understanding of natural law for the benefit of the individual and society. As director of the Institute of Science, Technology and Public Policy, a progressive policy think tank, Dr. Hagelin has successfully headed a nationwide effort to identify, scientifically verify, and promote cost-effective solutions to critical social problems in the fields of crime, health care, education, economy, energy, and the environment.

In recognition of his outstanding achievements, Dr. Hagelin was named winner of the prestigious Kilby Award, which honors scientists who have made major contributions to society through their applied research in the fields

of science and technology. The award recognized Dr. Hage-
lin as a scientist in the tradition of Einstein, Jeans, Bohr,
and Eddington.

We asked Dr. Hagelin to share his own passions and to
talk about the relationship between passion, consciousness,
and the unified field that underlies our universe.

"The most important key to success and happiness in my life
is experiencing unbounded awareness, the field of pure spirituality within, and identifying my awareness with the unified
field—the universal intelligence that governs the universe.
This brings immediate expansion, joy, pure creativity, and total support of nature for health and success and happiness in
life.

"I'm really blessed with a program that brings immediate
expansion, immediate bliss, and immediate contact with the
infinite. I'm fortunate to be a teacher of the Transcendental
Meditation (TM) program as taught by Maharishi Mahesh
Yogi. The TM program is the world's most widely practiced,
widely researched, and broadly prescribed technology for the
full development of human potential.

"In addition, I need purposeful activity that brings
evolution to humankind, activity that alleviates global
problems and suffering, and promotes peace in the world. I
need to see tangible results, tangible success in this and all my
projects.

"I'm passionate about peace, about ending this terrible legacy of human cruelty and warfare, as well as the deep igno-
rance that permits such life-afflicting behavior. I'm passionate
about education, especially education for enlightenment, a

new paradigm of education that involves full human potential and that develops the total brain.

"Modern education is really a travesty in that it develops a mere sliver of one's brain potential, and as a result, it deprives a human being of his or her natural capability of living enlightenment.

"I am a born teacher and I need to teach. The teacher always gains more than he gives. The way to understand anything most profoundly is to explain it to someone else, and that's the experience of every teacher. I teach graduate courses in unified quantum field theories. The way to really own the material is to impart that understanding to someone else, and somehow, magically almost, the material organizes itself more clearly and profoundly for the teacher.

"I love being with people who are evolving, who share this natural joy of life, and especially those who are enlightened, established in higher states of consciousness. The activities of such people are naturally evolutionary, life giving, bliss bestowing.

"I love speaking to large audiences, and the medium of live television, probably because it leverages one's impact and ability to reach large numbers of people and thus make a difference. I love art and music and being surrounded by inspiration and beauty.

"I love living in a dwelling built in accord with natural law, a dwelling designed for maximum, life-supporting, life-nourishing influence. Maharishi's Sthapatya Vedic architecture, which is more ancient and more complete than feng shui, is a tremendous blessing and a formula for success in itself.

"To understand passion is to get to the core nature of life, the very purpose of life, which is to progress and to evolve and grow toward fulfillment. If we're progressing and evolving, then we experience joy, energy, vitality, and health.

"Those activities through which we grow—through which we expand in knowledge, expand in power, expand in fulfillment—are the types of activities that bring us joy. If I'm passionate about something or you're passionate about something, it's because that something brings joy to us, nourishment to us—that activity is a path of evolution and expansion for us—expansion of knowledge, influence, power, and happiness.

"If you're not passionate about an activity, it means that activity isn't providing you with growth, satisfaction, joy, and expansion. Passion and success are inseparable to me. Passion is born of success—and the progress that comes with success.

"People are drawn to an activity because when they tasted that activity, they immediately experienced growth and progress in that direction. Typically, it's where their talent lies. It's a natural channel of creativity for them.

"Pursuit of passion is so basic to life, so intimate to life, that if you're not pursuing your passions, you're not going to be happy for long. You're not going to be able to sustain that direction for very long. Yet one does have control, to some extent, over what constitutes one's passion.

"What you put your attention on grows stronger in your life. You can culture an interest for something. You can develop a talent in an area, which then allows you to succeed in that area and thus enjoy progress, success, and evolution through that channel. That area will become more and more of a passion for you when your activity in that area rewards you with joy, progress, expansion, and evolution.

"People do have freedom—and it's probably the greatest

human freedom—over what they give their attention to. And that area will become more central, more important in their life. I would recommend everyone exercise that freedom—to put their attention on projects that are truly worthy, with the potential to bring maximum happiness and evolution to their life and to society as a whole.

"The more global and far-reaching the project, the more happiness and evolution that project could potentially bring. We have control over what might become a passion for us, and that's an important freedom we exercise. But there are obviously constraints on what could ever become our passion, based upon our core predispositions and genetic makeup.

"Probably, although I enjoy art, painting will never become a passion for me: I am so utterly lacking in talent in that area that an effort in that direction would almost certainly meet with more frustration than joy. If I had some talent, if I were even moderately talented, I could nurture that talent, enjoy initial spurts of progress, and that could ultimately grow into a passion for me.

"So we have some control, but there are constraints based upon our own individual natures. Not everyone is going to be a great teacher. Not everyone is going to be a great politician. In my life, I made choices to develop new areas, new passions that weren't, frankly, that natural to me—talents I wasn't born with. I was not born a quantum physicist: I was born an engineer.

"When it came to classical physics, the laws of mechanics, I didn't have to study them. I knew them, they were in my bones, they were part of my genetic makeup. But when it came to quantum mechanics, I had entered a strange new realm that was absolutely nonintuitive to me.

"I should say, in fairness, quantum mechanics is counter-intuitive to most people. You have to rely solely on your mathematical abilities to delve into these abstract realms for which our intuition provides no guidance. And I wasn't a born mathematician. I had to really develop those skills over a period of years before I gained a natural fluency with the quantum world and began to tackle problems in that world with increasing ease—and finally I gained some spark of fulfillment.

"It took time to develop that new channel of creative intelligence, that new channel of progress and satisfaction. It took time to build that new passion.

"Moving into social policy is the second example of creating a new passion, of developing myself in an area where I wasn't endowed with God-given talent, for the sake of the higher calling of service to humanity. Public policy didn't light my fire before I undertook this calling to evolve better principles and policies to govern our country and the world.

"I dove into the area of public policy, health care reform, etc., and relatively quickly, in comparison to quantum physics, found myself in a position of being able to make important, original contributions to those fields. It's not rocket science, you could say. It's not quantum physics.

"It didn't take that long to expose the fallacies of our current policies in such areas as defense, which is based on offense, or health care, which is based on disease care, and so forth—and to construct more life-supporting policies that are in harmony with natural law and make more efficient, compassionate use of our precious resources.

"So this is another example of how my deepest sense of responsibility caused me to actually nurture and build a whole new passion, which then became the driving force of my life for quite a few years.

"What I came to learn after fifteen years of higher education is that the material universe is built upon the nonmaterial quantum mechanical world of abstract intelligence that underlies it. The exploration of deeper levels of natural law at the atomic and nuclear and subnuclear levels was probing deeper levels of intelligence in nature that were far beyond the realm of material existence.

"Ultimately, the discovery of the unified field, or heterotic superstring, was a discovery of a field of pure intelligence whose nature was not material, but pure, self-interacting consciousness. So physics, in effect, had discovered consciousness at the foundation of material existence.

"I wanted to know the nature of that consciousness, and it was through Maharishi's programs, through his techniques for the development of consciousness, that I experienced the reality of what that field of consciousness is. I discovered for myself that human intelligence, at its core foundation, is universal intelligence, and at that level you and I and everyone and everything in the universe are one.

"We are united at our core, and that truth, that ultimate truth of the unity of life, is the most precious and crucially important understanding to emerge in this scientific age. This is the same reality that has been celebrated since time immemorial in all the great spiritual traditions of the world. But now this same truth is open to objective verification through the empirical approach of modern physics, and open to personal verification through the experiential approach of consciousness, and specifically for me, through the very universal

and powerful technologies of Maharishi's Vedic science, including the Transcendental Meditation program.

"My most ardent desire today is to see an end to the sense-
less violence and continual legacy of war that has confronted
humankind for so many, countless generations and to bring
lasting peace to the world on the basis of the emerging global
understanding of the essential unity of life.

"When all of us can own that vision, when all of us reading
this can deeply understand and experience the unity of life,
that unity will be far more easily understood and assimilated
by the billions of citizens of our global family. We are almost
at the point where these words, where the ultimate reality of
the unity of life, is resonating with people, beginning to make
sense to people.

"We're not quite there, and it's important that we nucleate
the transition, that we precipitate the transformation by
bringing this core understanding and experience to as many
people as possible. And from that understanding and experience of unity, real, lasting peace will inevitably dawn in the
world today.

"There's really no limit to human potential, and there's no
limit to what we can effortlessly achieve. The secret is to align
human intelligence with the vast, organizing intelligence of
nature that governs the universe and upholds millions of spe-
cies here on earth and trillions throughout the universe.

"By aligning our desires with the natural evolutionary flow
of universal intelligence, virtually any impulse of thought can
meet with tremendous success. Aligning individual intelligence
with nature's intelligence is what is called enlightenment.

"Developing the total brain and rising to higher states of
consciousness is absolutely key to achieving individual fulfill-

ment and is the key to contributing maximum to the evolution of society toward an enlightened society—a unified field–based civilization of peace, prosperity, and harmony in the family of nations."

What were the key lessons from this interview about living your passion?

1. The core nature of life is to progress and evolve toward fulfillment.

2. When we're progressing and evolving, we experience joy, energy, vitality, and health.

3. Activities through which we grow, through which we expand in knowledge, power, fulfillment—that type of activity brings joy.

4. When we're passionate about something, it's because it brings us joy, because that activity is a path of evolution and expansion for us.

5. If you're not passionate about an activity, that activity isn't bringing you growth and expansion.

6. Passion is born of success and the progress that comes with success.

7. Pursuit of passion is so basic to life that if you're not pursuing your passions, you're not going to be happy for long and you're not going to be able to sustain that direction for very long.

8. You have control over what might become a passion for you, within the constraints of your core predispositions and genetic makeup. You can culture an interest for something, or develop a talent in an area, which allows you to succeed in that area, and that area will become more of a passion.

9. The greatest human freedom is the freedom over what you give your attention to. That area will become more central, more important to your life.

10. Your deepest sense of responsibility can cause you to nurture and build whole new passions.

11. The material universe is built on the nonmaterial quantum-mechanical world of abstract intelligence that underlies it.

12. There is no limit to human potential and no limit to what we can effortlessly achieve. The secret is to align human intelligence with the vast, organizing intelligence of nature.

13. By aligning our desires with the natural evolutionary flow of universal intelligence, any impulse of thought can meet with tremendous success. Aligning individual intelligence with nature's intelligence is what is called enlightenment.

Epilogue

As we mentioned at the beginning of the book, it has taken more than thirty years for the two of us to truly align our lives with our passions. For us it's been a journey, as it surely has and will be for you.

Sometimes we were perfectly aligned, sometimes we were way off track. What has become clear is that being aligned leads to a life of joy, fullness, and delight. When we have been off track, it was miserable.

Along the way we discovered that support is essential. No matter how much we wanted to choose for our passions, sometimes those old beliefs and concepts reared their ugly heads. If it weren't for our mentors and teachers, we wouldn't be living the extraordinary lives we do today.

So, we encourage you to seek out help and support. No successful person has *ever* made it on his or her own. Find the resources, mentors, and teachers who can help you live the life you deserve to live. We've listed some we know and trust in the resources section at the back of this book. Make the decision to be open to learning and receiving help. It can make all the difference.

Most of all, keep taking The Passion Test regularly and enjoy your trip down the cosmic highway. Come back to this page when you need to quickly reference your driver's manual on the journey:

Discovering gifts—When you give attention to the good in your life, you will create more good. When you discover the gifts in every moment, in every situation, in every person you meet, your life will be filled with gifts.

Give what you want to receive—The way to have happiness is to give what you want to have. On the relative plane, life is like a mirror. Whatever you do, that is what you will receive.

Action engages attention—It is not the action that achieves the result. Things will almost certainly not turn out the way you plan. But by taking action you keep your attention engaged with fulfilling your intention. It is your attention that creates the outcome.

Nature's Guidance System—Nature will guide you every step of the way when you are open to her messages. When you feel expanded, take action, move forward, and enjoy the process of achievement. When you feel contracted, stop, take a break, rest, reflect, and enjoy the process of coming back to your self.

Surrender—What can I do today to resign as general manager of the universe so I can allow what I am supposed to be doing? Remarkable things happen when you surrender.

Set sail when the sailing is good—Timing is everything. When you are beginning a journey, it's good to check with the weatherman before you start. When you are beginning an important new phase of your life, it's good to check with a competent Jyotishi to begin at a time when the going is most likely to be good.

Failure is not an option—When you are truly aligned with your passions, nothing can stop you.

Three obstacles on the path—There are only three obstacles to living a passionate life: false beliefs, false concepts, and false ideas. When you argue with reality, you lose, and only 100 percent of the time. When you discover you are making choices in favor of something other than what's most important to you, investigate your thinking. The Work of Byron Katie is one of the most powerful tools we've found for undoing limiting beliefs.

No Tension—Acting from the state of No Tension is the key to performing action that produces powerful results. This state of No Tension is the inner state of wholeness, of calmness. When the mind is calm, then inspiration is natural.

Help Others to Help Yourself—To have everything you want in your life, help others get what they want for their lives.

The Speed of Trust—Trust is central to living a passionate life—trusting that you live in a benevolent universe and creating trust in your relationships with others. In relationships, high trust makes things happen quickly and dramatically lowers costs.

The Bliss Is Always There—At your source, you are full. Attachment to false beliefs or ideas can prevent you from experiencing the bliss that is always there. Go into the pain, feel it fully, and you will rediscover the bliss.

Follow the bread crumbs—Your passions are leading you to discover who you really are. Take The Passion Test as often as you want, and not less than every six months. Each time you will discover more about yourself.

Enduring success—As you become clearer and clearer about what really matters to you, your passions will change less over time. Your core passions can find fulfillment through many different channels. Keep taking The Passion Test regularly, consistently choose in favor of your passions, and your core passions will naturally emerge.

United at our core—At the deepest level we are all connected. The more fully you connect with your own passions, the more deeply you will be able to connect with others.

Whatever you choose to do, remember the power and strength of love. The things you love the most, those things we call passions, are drawing you irresistibly on to the fulfillment of your destiny.

We leave you with this thought:

Passion is born of love.
Love is the perfection of the divine in us.
Love lives, breathes
and finds expression through us
and fills us with the fire of passion.
Fulfillment arises from love
and through love.

Let us live in love, for love's sake.
Let us be in love
and share our love
in the service of our common destiny.
Let passion emerge from us as love,
in the service of humanity.

Acknowledgments

As with every book, many people have made this one possible. Our partners at *Healthy Wealthy nWise*, Ric and Liz Thompson, have been incredible. Every crazy idea we have that makes at least a modicum of sense, they have supported. They chose to share their magazine with us and then worked shoulder to shoulder as together we have created a unique online resource that allows everyday people to spend time with and learn from some of the most amazing people in the world. Ric and Liz, thank you first and foremost for your friendship and for creating the online systems that allow so many people to gain the knowledge they need to live their destinies.

Mark Victor Hansen and Robert G. Allen, thank you for who you are. You showed us that the door marked Security isn't secure at all, and the door marked Freedom is a lot more fun, if a bit hair-raising at times. And thank you for being open to our idea of putting *enlightened* and *millionaire* together, so we can all begin to realize that spirituality and wealth are complementary, not mutually exclusive, ways of living life.

Harv Eker, Jack Canfield, Paul Scheele, Pete Bisonnette, Bill

Harris, Michael Beckwith, Byron Katie, Jay Abraham, Pankaj and Smita Naram, Bill Bauman, and Tom Painter, we are so grateful for your friendship and for your generosity in sharing your knowledge, your experience, and your wisdom.

Marci Shimoff, what an extraordinary friend and counselor you have been. Your love, wisdom, and practical advice have been indispensable. Thank you for reminding us of who we are.

Bill Levacy, thank you for your profound Jyotish guidance and amazing ability to take the simple words "intention, attention, no tension" and give so much clarity to them that our lives and our readers' lives will forever be transformed.

Sylva Dvorak, Pat Burns, and Melony Malouf, thank you for being the best of friends—always there, always ready to support us when we really need it. You are so special to us.

Bonnie Solow, you are the best agent in the world. Thank you for being such a good friend, for pushing us to be our best, and for representing our interests with such integrity. We cherish our relationship.

Christina Collins Hill, your Jyotish skills have been so important in helping us "avert the danger which has not yet come." Thank you for your continued love and support in all that we do.

Chris Strodder, thank you for your patience in reading and rereading the original version of this book so many times. Your suggestions, questions, and comments have made the final version so much richer.

Liz Howard, you are a miracle worker. Thank you for doing such a beautiful job in designing the original edition of the book and for doing it in record time. George Foster, what a treat you are to work with, play with, and laugh with. Your sense of humor combined with your incredible design skills have made you one of our ideal partners. We are excited to help the world know you're the one to go to when they need an amazing book cover.

From Janet: I'm so thankful to all the great Masters who opened their hearts and minds, and in many cases, their homes, so I could both fulfill my passions and share their wisdom with so many.

To my Angel group, Mo, Sue, Suzanne, Cindy, Tony, Jerrie, Deb Sue, and Sandy, thank you for always being my cheering squad! Even if your minds couldn't always wrap your arms around what I was up to, your hearts always did.

To Mickey and Johnny, my dear sister and brother, what a blessing you are in my life. It's so amazing to know that whatever happens, you will always be there for me. Thank you for your encouragement, for your love, and for helping to pick me up when the road got tough.

Christian Seaton and Sandy Magram, thank you for being the best friends a girl could ever want, all these many years. Radhika Schwartz, Martin Gluckman, and Krishna, thank you for pointing me in the direction of the wisest people on the planet.

Martin, I'm so grateful to you for traveling with me on parts of my journey. Juliann Jannus, thank you for your flexibility in leaving your job to travel across the world with me, and thank you for getting me started on my video career.

Debra Sue Poneman, you started me on this journey, almost thirty years ago. Thank you for your inspiration, your wisdom, and for making the world of transformation look like so much fun!

To Ashoklal, Bindu, Krishna, and Devu, and to Kannan, Amita, and the rest of my Indian family, thank you for taking such good care of me and making sure I had a home away from home.

Glory be Chris . . . what haven't we been through together?! Thank you for teaching me that "if it isn't fun, I don't want to play." Thank you as well for your incredible ability to bring out the greatness in everyone around you. It's an honor to be your best friend and business partner.

To my dear parents and beloved Margie, I am what I am because of you. Thank you for pushing me to be my own person.

From Chris: My dear beloved Doe, what a blessing you are in my life. Thank you for your patience with me through the late nights, early mornings, and weekends it took to get this book done. Your continued love and support mean everything to me.

Mom and Erich, thank you for showering me with your love. Mom, thank you for always encouraging me to follow my own direction, even when you thought it was completely nuts.

Dear Dad. What a life we had together, huh? Thank you for allowing me to feel so loved. This book is as much yours as it is mine. Thank you for showing me what courage really looks like.

Rolf and Renee Erickson, what amazing friends you are. Thank you for your excellent feedback. Bob and Patricia Oates, I am so grateful for you both. Bob and Rolf, thank you for sharing so many incredible, passionate adventures with me, so I actually have an idea what it means to live passionately.

Mark Schoenfeld, thank you for your friendship and for reminding me of what is real. To all my buddies on the Purusha Program, in the United States, Europe, and in the high mountains of the Himalayas, thank you for your silence, your dedication, and the powerful effect of coherence you are having on the world.

And Janet, what a remarkable teacher you are. You have helped me transform my life into more than I could ever have dreamed. It's so unbelievable to know there is someone who will never give up on me, who I can always depend on, who will do whatever it takes. You are my inspiration, my best friend, and my perfect business partner.

And lastly, on behalf of both of us, we cannot begin to give words to the deep gratitude we feel to His Holiness Maharishi Mahesh Yogi for giving us the direct experience and understanding of the most fundamental nature of reality. We feel deeply blessed.

About the Authors

Cofounders of online magazine *Healthy Wealthy nWise* and partners in Enlightened Alliances, a marketing consulting firm, Chris and Janet Attwood regularly spend time with some of the greatest transformational leaders, interviewing them on their passions.

Their Passion Series interviews have helped thousands of people learn the principles that lead to a passionate life. They've interviewed people like T. Harv Eker, Neale Donald Walsch, Byron Katie, Stephen R. Covey, David Lynch, Dr. Wayne Dyer, John Gray, Willie Nelson, Rhonda Byrne, and many others.

Chris and Janet were once married, but are no longer, yet they remain best friends and business partners. After many successful years in the corporate world, they gave up the security of their well-paid jobs to partner with Mark Victor Hansen and Robert Allen to create the Enlightened Millionaire Program.

They are founding members of Jack Canfield's Transformational Leadership Council and active members of Marshall Thurber's Positive Deviant Network.

Janet Attwood is a master communicator and connector. She has always had the gift of connecting with people, no matter what their status or position. From the influential and powerful to the rich and famous to the Saints of India, Nepal, the Philippines, and elsewhere, to lepers and AIDS patients and anyone who is seeking to live their destiny, Janet bonds with everyone.

She has been the top salesperson at every company she has worked at over the past twenty years and ran the marketing division of Books Are Fun, at the time the third-largest book buyer in the United States. In the year after her division posted record sales, Books Are Fun was sold to Reader's Digest for $360 million.

Janet was awarded the key to the city of Miami and has been nominated for the President's Volunteer Service Award for her work with homeless women in transition.

She has created the first-ever transformational series, called *The Empowered Women's Series.* This powerful program is played at homeless shelters around the United States and features re-nowned female transformational leaders including Byron Katie, Marci Shimoff, Rickie Byars Beckwith, Cynthia Kersey, Lynne Twist, Jan Stringer, Lisa Nichols, Dr. Sue Morter, and Janet.

Janet has been practicing the Transcendental Meditation program for more than thirty-five years and is a facilitator of The Work of Byron Katie.

Chris Attwood is an expert in the field of consciousness. For thirty-five years he has studied and explored the field of human consciousness. In the eighties he spent more than ten years in deep meditation and has extensively studied the Vedic tradition of India.

He has also put his theoretical knowledge to practice. Chris is skilled at consultative sales and management. Over the past thirty years he has been president, chief operating officer, general manager, or CEO of ten companies. He has sold millions of dollars of consulting and training to organizations like Dell Computer, Royal Bank of Canada, Sprint, Ford Motor Company, Mellon Bank, and others.

Janet and Chris are committed to the experience and expression of the unlimited potential of the heart and mind. They teach, and their daily practice is what it means to live a life of unconditional love.

Resources

RESOURCES FROM THE BOOK

As we said in the Epilogue, having support has been critical to our ability to align our lives with our passions. On this page and in the section titled "Other Resources" that follows you will find people and programs we know and trust that can provide you with the support you need to live your passionate life.

Healthy Wealthy nWise

Not only does this online magazine provide useful, helpful articles each month, you can listen to the live interviews we do with some of the most successful people in the world about how they discovered and live their passions. In the past, these interviews have included people such as: Stephen R. Covey, Willie Nelson, David Lynch, Wayne Dyer, Robert Kiyosaki, Byron Katie, Barbara DeAngelis, Stedman Graham, John Gray, Rhonda Byrne, T. Harv Eker, Neale Donald Walsch, and many others. To become an *HWnW* subscriber and register to listen to the Passion interview calls, go to:

www.healthywealthynwise.com/interview

Chris and Janet's Websites

To learn more about us and explore the tools we've made available to support our readers in living their passions, go to:

www.thepassiontest.com

To take The Passion Test online, go to:

www.passiontestonline.com

To get a copy of our ebook, *From Sad to Glad – 7 Steps to Facing Change with Love and Power,* go to:

www.thepassiontest.com/fromsadtoglad

For information on becoming a certified Passion Test facilitator, go to:

www.thepassiontest.com/cert

And if you are interested in our other work you can go to:

www.janetattwood.com
www.stayinginlove.com
www.enlightenedalliances.com

Interview Guests' Websites

You have read some of the extraordinary interviews we conducted with Debbie Ford, Richard Paul Evans, Stephen M. R. Covey, Jay Abraham, Marci Shimoff, and Dr. John Hagelin. Here's where you can learn more about each of them:

Debbie Ford:	**www.debbieford.com** or
	www.bestyearofyourlife.com
Richard Paul Evans:	**www.richardpaulevans.com** or
	www.thechristmasboxhouse.org

Stephen M. R. Covey: **www.coveylink.com**
Jay Abraham: **www.abraham.com**
Marci Shimoff: **www.marcishimoff.com** or
  www.happyfornoreason.com
Dr. John Hagelin: **www.istpp.org** or **www.tm.org** or
  www.permanentpeace.org or
  www.hagelin.org

From Our Stories

If you were fascinated by some of the stories in *The Passion Test*, some of these people have websites where you can learn more about them and their work.

Byron Katie: **www.thepassiontest.com/thework**
Rhonda Byrne: **www.thepassiontest.com/thesecret**
Lynn Carnes: **www.thepassiontest.com/badboss**
Karen Nelson Bell: **www.thepassiontest.com/**
  karennelsonbell
Unleash America's
Passion: **www.thepassiontest.com/unleash**
Power Behind **www.thepassiontest.com/**
the Passion: **powerbehindthepassion**

Jyotish Resources

In chapter 10 we shared our "secret weapon," the science of timing. If you would like more information about this fascinating subject, here are two resources we recommend:

Bill Levacy: **www.thepassiontest.com/levacy**
Christina Collins: **www.thepassiontest.com/**
  christinacollins

OTHER RESOURCES

Expanding Awareness, Deepening Your Experience of Life

Transcendental Meditation (TM)—We have both been practicing this powerfully effective program of deep meditation for over thirty years. We consider it the foundation on which everything else is built. It's simple, it's easy to do, it works, and it complements every other practice. Over six hundred scientific studies have been done on the benefits of TM. Be prepared to make an investment that will return to you many times over in innumerable ways.

www.thepassiontest.com/tm

The Work of Byron Katie—Byron Katie (affectionately known as Katie) is a remarkable woman who "woke up" to reality many years ago. In the process, she experienced an incredibly powerful and easy process of investigation that she now teaches throughout the world. The Work will allow you to systematically and effortlessly unravel the concepts that keep you from living your greatness. It was a huge turning point in allowing us to deal with our challenges.

www.thepassiontest.com/thework

The Sedona Method—We've all been told the value of "letting go." The Sedona Method is a simple yet profound practice for doing just that. There is no limit to what you can accomplish or create in your life when you are able to truly let go of the emotions and concepts that hold you back.

www.thepassiontest.com/sedona

Centerpointe Research Institute—In the seventies, research found that sine waves in various forms could produce predictable changes in brain wave patterns. Bill Harris of Centerpointe Research used this knowledge to create the unique Holosync audio technology that creates the brain wave patterns associated with deep meditation. Holosync users report a broad spectrum of benefits in all areas of their lives. If you have had trouble with traditional meditation practices, this may be the solution you've been looking for.

  www.thepassiontest.com/centerpointe

Building the Foundation of Self-Knowledge

Jack Canfield's Private Mentorship Program—Jack Canfield, cocreator of the Chicken Soup for the Soul series is one of the best trainers in the world today. He will take you to new places in yourself and allow you to see the greatness in you. If you can't do any other trainings this year, do Jack's.

  www.thepassiontest.com/canfield

Robert Scheinfeld's Busting Loose from the Money Game—If your aim is to go beyond creating wealth to breaking free from the money game, you have to take this program. "Secrets" is a bit overused in the marketing world, but this program really will unveil some core secrets about the nature of reality. Chris took this program and said it turned his world upside down. Prepare to have your mind blown. When you're finished, you'll understand what real freedom is and be starting to live it.

  www.thepassiontest.com/bustingloose

Agape International Spiritual Center—Founded by Dr. Michael Beckwith in 1986 with fifteen members, today there are over ten thousand members and thousands attend services each Sunday. Nondenominational, Agape is an experience you don't want to miss if you are ever in Los Angeles, California. You'll experience the most inspiring music, loving community, and sermons by Rev. Michael, which will transfix, motivate, and transform you. Words cannot begin to describe the experience of Agape. You have to experience it.

www.thepassiontest.com/agape

The Kabbalah Centre—You've heard about the Kabbalah Centre from the news articles about their famous students. What you may not know is that Kabbalah's ancient teachings are immensely practical and applicable to building the life you have dreamed about.

www.thepassiontest.com/kabbalah

Bill Bauman—We sometimes refer to him as "the enlightened Mister Rogers." *Funny, perceptive, inspiring,* and *thought provoking* are all words that describe Bill. His courses, retreats, and community of friends can be an incredible support when you need to surround yourself with people who will encourage you to fully express who you are.

www.thepassiontest.com/billbauman

The Unstoppable Cynthia Kersey—She wrote the book on being *Unstoppable*, she is mobilizing the unstoppable women of the world, and she is the living embodiment of what it means to be unstoppable.

www.thepassiontest.com/unstoppable

Dr. John DeMartini's Breakthrough Experience—John DeMartini's trainings are worth attending just for the pleasure of sitting with such a brilliant mind. From quantum physics to the mechanisms by which you create your reality, John will hold you spellbound. Then be prepared to do some serious inner work. Expect to come out of his courses transformed. You will be.

www.thepassiontest.com/demartini

Money and You: Excellerated Business Schools—Marshall Thurber created Money and You over thirty years ago. It is now run by D. C. Cordova and is still one of the most powerful courses available. While the title is about money, the content is a series of experiential games that will show you who you really are. Tony Robbins, Robert Kiyosaki, T. Harv Eker, Jack Canfield, Mark Victor Hansen, Spencer Johnson, and many others have gone through this course before achieving their success. Think *you* might learn something there?

www.thepassiontest.com/moneyandyou

Attracting Perfect Customers—Jan Stringer and Alan Hickman will teach you a systematic process for attracting whomever you want into your life, from perfect customers to the perfect relationship to the perfect employee to the perfect business partner. We use their process with every major initiative we take.

www.thepassiontest.com/perfectcustomers

Destiny Training Systems—Do you know you live in an abundant universe, but don't know how to access that abundance? Scott deMoulin's Destiny Training will show you how.

Teaching practical strategies for achieving true inner and outer wealth, Scott and his partner, Dallyce Brisbin, have a huge following of raving fans.

www.thepassiontest.com/destinytraining

James Ray International—"Balance is bogus! Harmony is what leads to happiness and real wealth," says master trainer James Ray. His Journey of Power course draws on his broad experience in traditional business and the ancient cultures of Peru, Egypt, and the Amazon jungle. He considers himself a "practical mystic" and in our experience he is a trainer who will challenge you, entertain you, sometimes shock you, and by one means or another, wake you up to the power that resides inside you.

www.thepassiontest.com/jamesray

The Happy Healthy Wealthy Game and the Ultimate Game of Life—Jim Bunch started his career as part of the lead team for Tony Robbins, enrolling students in Tony Robbins seminars. He then became one of the founders of Bamboo.com and retired for a while after the company went public. Now he has created the acclaimed Happy Healthy Wealthy Game and the Ultimate Game of Life. Both of these coaching experiences can completely transform your experience of life.

www.thepassiontest.com/jimbunch

Creating Power—Over the past twenty years Karim Hajee has been teaching his amazing Creating Power System that has helped thousands of people change their lives in ways they never thought possible. He learned how to tap into his subconscious mind and developed the Creating Power System from his mother when he was a teenager living in Kenya, East Africa. She in turn was taught by her mother who discovered this system while she lived in India. The Creating Power System can be a powerfully effective method for creating the life you want.

www.thepassiontest.com/creatingpower

Creating Wealth

T. Harv Eker's Millionaire Mind Intensive—Harv wrote the book on having a millionaire mind (*Secrets of the Millionaire Mind*), and he's one of the best trainers we've ever experienced. His courses are fun, challenging, and incredibly rewarding. You will be an empowered, fearless person when you emerge. Get a copy of Harv's great book. If you're just getting started on the path to financial wealth, this is the place to begin.

www.thepassiontest.com/eker

Alex Mandossian—Alex left a six-figure income as a corporate marketing executive to follow his passions. Today he enjoys a much higher income working from home. He is one of the most effective trainers we know. If you are committed to monetizing your passions, spend some time with Alex.

www.thepassiontest.com/alexm

Robert Allen's Enlightened Wealth Institute—We can't say enough good about our former partner. Popularly known as the protégé program, the Enlightened Wealth Institute provides practical, hands-on courses, and will teach you the ins and outs of creating wealth through real estate, stocks, Internet marketing, and "infopreneuring" (marketing information).

www.thepassiontest.com/emi

Raymond Aaron's Monthly Mentor—Famed for his financial success in Canada, author of *Chicken Soup for the Parent's Soul* and *Chicken Soup for the Canadian Soul*, Raymond Aaron's Monthly Mentor program is not to be missed. Every month he interviews incredible people from Robert Kiyosaki to Mark Victor Hansen to Brian Tracy to Randy Gage, and gets them to spill their guts about what it takes to be successful. Raymond's interviews have created a loyal following for good reason.

www.thepassiontest.com/aaron

One Coach—The founders of One Coach, John Assaraf and Murray Smith, have made millions, repeatedly, in a variety of businesses. Now they are focused on helping the small business owner and entrepreneur with under $1 million in sales. Their program will coach you through the obstacles and challenges while helping you identify the opportunities. What we love is the holistic approach they take to your success.

www.thepassiontest.com/onecoach

BNI (Business Networks International)—Founded by Dr. Ivan Misner, over twenty years ago, when he wanted to generate more business for his consulting practice, BNI has grown to over one hundred thousand members and almost five thousand chapters. Allowing one member of each "flavor" (doctor, lawyer, hairstylist, chiropractor, etc.) per chapter, BNI members come together regularly to share referrals with each other.

Based on the philosophy that "givers gain," last year alone BNI members exchanged over 2 million referrals and generated almost a billion U.S. dollars in business for each other.

www.thepassiontest.com/bni

Stephen Pierce—If your path to wealth is through the Internet, prepare to learn from one of the best. From search engine strategies to launching a book to eBay auctions to getting publicity, Stephen is one of the leaders in the field of internet marketing. When you go to this site, we encourage you to stay open. Stephen is a great person and you can learn a great deal from him about monetizing your passions by adapting his methods to your own style.

www.thepassiontest.com/pierce

Success University—This is one place you can go to get trained by the greatest mentors on creating wealth in the world. You'll take courses with Jim Rohn, Zig Ziglar, Brian Tracy, Les Brown, Jay Abraham, and many more. This unique resource is based on a network marketing model so you can learn and earn at the same time.

www.thepassiontest.com/successu

Wildly Wealthy Women—This incredibly successful program from Down Under is soon coming to North America. Sandy Forster and Dymphna Boholt have created a program exclusively for women, teaching them asset management, nothing-down real estate strategies, safe stock market investment strategies, and a host of other practical skills in a safe environment created by women for women.

www.thepassiontest.com/wildlywealthy

Health

Maharishi Ayurveda in Bad Ems, Germany—Come discover why Chris and his wife, Doris, spend three to six months in Bad Ems. The Ayurvedic Health Center is one of the top spas in Europe, having won numerous awards. They provide personal care, very comfortable accommodations in the historic four-star Haecker Kurhotel, and surroundings that are nothing short of sublime. Come in late spring, summer, or early fall, and you may run into Chris and Doris strolling along lighted walkways in the part adjacent to the Lahn River, and, if you're really lucky, you might find Janet there visiting them as well.

   www.thepassiontest.com/badems

The Healing Codes—Twelve years of prayers were answered when the healing system he now calls the Healing Codes appeared to Dr. Alex Loyd and cured his wife's severe depression when nothing else would. As he applied the Healing Codes to the psychological and emotional issues of his clients, he was taken aback when they started reporting their recovery from serious health issues like multiple sclerosis, leukemia, Lou Gehrig's disease, and others. Dr. Loyd is a wonderful, loving man. If health is an issue, the Healing Codes could create a miracle in your life.

   www.thepassiontest.com/healingcode

Morter Health Systems—Dr. Ted Morter Jr. has become a legend in the chiropractic industry. His BEST system (Bio-Energetic Synchronization Technique) has performed miracles for people suffering from illnesses of all kinds. His sons,

Dr. Ted Jr. and Dr. Tom, and his daughter, Dr. Sue Morter, are powerhouses in their own rights.

www.thepassiontest.com/morter

Ayushakti: Dr. Pankaj and Smita Naram—You've read some of his story in *The Passion Test*. Mother Teresa praised him for his work, he has treated over 400,000 patients with outstanding results, and he has Ayurvedic centers in twelve countries around the world. Dr. Naram comes to the U.S. twice a year and travels to Europe, Australia, and other parts of the globe regularly. He is a remarkable man and an incredible source of healing knowledge.

www.thepassiontest.com/naram

Master Stephen Co and Pranic Healing—Master Co is the author of *Your Hands Can Heal You*. He has been praised by Dr. Deepak Chopra, Marianne Williamson, Carolyn Myss, Mark Victor Hansen, and many others for the power of his healing work. His active practice is teaching people how to heal themselves.

www.thepassiontest.com/stephenco

Sri Sunil Das—Janet described some of the remarkable experiences she had with Sri Sunil Das in part 1 of *The Passion Test*. Royalty, politicians, leading musicians, actors, and actresses, as well as tens of thousands of Indians with all kinds of maladies, come to Sri Sunil Das for healing. He is humble, kind, fun, and insists all the healing that happens through him is "God's will."

www.thepassiontest.com/sunildas

Master Chunyi Lin—Author of the number one bestseller *Born a Healer*, Chunyi insists that anyone can heal themselves. He is a master of the ancient arts of Qigong, and his book is a good place to start in understanding how to heal yourself. His Spring Forest Qigong is offered through Learning Strategies Corporation (see "Other Resources" below) as a powerful self-study program.

www.thepassiontest.com/chunyi

Amazon Herbs—"More than a company. A way of being in the world" is Amazon Herbs' motto. How often do you connect with a company that is committed to your personal health and lifestyle goals? A company that honors nature and indigenous culture? A company that lives a successful model of ecological prosperity every day and is the best at what they do? Amazon Herbs brings the healing medicinal herbs of the Amazon rain forest into your life.

www.thepassiontest.com/amazon

Relationships

Dr. John Gray—What is there to say about the man who wrote the bestselling relationship book of all time, *Men Are from Mars, Women Are from Venus*. John offers a wide variety of resources to support men and women in creating healthy, fulfilling relationships.

www.thepassiontest.com/marsvenus

Gay and Katie Hendricks—Cofounders of the Spiritual Cinema Circle, Gay and Katie have been supporting the creation of loving, fulfilling relationships in everyone who connects with them since they fell in love over twenty-five years ago. They have trained coaches throughout the world to bring hope, love, and the experience of unity to people everywhere.

www.thepassiontest.com/hendricks

Paul and Layne Cutright—Paul and Layne, bestselling authors, coaches and teachers, have been in a romantic and creative partnership since 1976. They have taught thousands of people the world over their secrets and strategies for successful relationships at home and in business.

www.healthywealthynwise.com/paulandlayne

Stephany Crowley's E-Dating Secrets—Internet dating is becoming one of the best ways to find your perfect partner. After all, Chris found his wife through the Internet. But it can be scary, uncertain, and a mammoth waste of time if you don't know what you're doing. Stephany wrote the book on *E-Dating Secrets*, and her programs can make you an Internet dating expert in no time.

www.thepassiontest.com/e-datingexperts

Family and Kids

Lisa Nichols's Motivating the Teen Spirit—Lisa has worked with over fifty thousand at-risk teens and helped more than two thousand avert suicide. She is one of the most powerful, warm, straightforward speakers and trainers we have met. You may have seen her in *The Secret*. If you have teens, you will want to connect with Lisa.

www.thepassiontest.com/teens

SuperCamp and Quantum Learning Network—SuperCamp has become famous for its powerful effect on kids and parents alike. It is based on concepts that make learning fun and easy, along with positive peer support and carefully orchestrated environmental factors. The use of metaphors like board breaking and ropes courses help students surpass barriers that hold them back. SuperCamp is ideal for kids and families to do together. Programs are offered throughout the United States and worldwide.

www.thepassiontest.com/supercamp

Personal Growth

Learning Strategies Corporation—Paul Scheele and Pete Bisonnette have created powerful tools for learning a variety of useful subjects using accelerated learning, preconscious processing, and neurolinguistic programming. Their products are outstanding. From Spring Forest Qigong to Diamond Feng Shui to PhotoReading to accessing your Genius Mind, to their Memory Optimizer, to just about any area you want to improve in, Learning Strategies has some of the best learning tools available anywhere.

www.thepassiontest.com/learningstrategies

ConsciousOne—Want access to incredible authors and transformational leaders? At ConsciousOne you can read articles, listen to recordings, and purchase products from people like Neale Donald Walsch, Dr. Wayne Dyer, Doreen Virtue, Sylvia Browne, Gay and Katie Hendricks, Barbara Marx Hubbard, and Jean Houston.

www.thepassiontest.com/consciousone

SelfGrowth.com—This is another mother lode of resources in the field of personal growth and development. Among many other things, you'll be able to get founder David Riklan's compilation of *Self Improvement: The Top 101 Experts that Help Us Improve Our Lives.* There are articles, event calendars, and much more at this very useful website.

www.thepassiontest.com/selfgrowth

Spiritual Cinema Circle—Receive inspirational, uplifting films every month as a member of Spiritual Cinema Circle. These are chosen from the best short and feature films shown at festivals around the world, and most, while excellent, you would never see otherwise. Every month includes at least one full-length feature along with several shorter, outstanding films.

www.thepassiontest.com/scc

Lefkoe Institute—From overcoming your fear of speaking to facing change to becoming a better parent to improving your golf game, Morty Lefkoe has created powerful processes for eliminating the beliefs that hold you back. Morty and his certified facilitators have had incredible success working with people with a wide variety of issues including eating disorders, depression, violent behavior, and stress, among many others.

www.thepassiontest.com/lefkoe

CoachVille—The largest association/network of coaches in the world, CoachVille brings together over forty thousand coaches. If you're interested in becoming a coach or connecting with coaches, this is the place to go.

www.thepassiontest.com/coachville

Doing Life! International—A 2004 study documented that her programs had saved state of New York taxpayers over $1 billion. Dr. Cheryl Clark has spent thirty years applying the wisdom of R. Buckminster Fuller to social situations through Social Synergetics. The Social Synergetics model for successful living integrates physical, mental, emotional, and spiritual components of human existence and offers a groundbreaking framework for lives and relationships that are vital, nourishing, creative, and joyful.

   www.thepassiontest.com/doinglife

When Just a Book Isn't Enough

Take The Passion Test Online:

**For thirty days, use the tools from this book in an
easy, fun, and powerful online format
to keep your life aligned with your passions and
your success expanding every single day.**

www.passiontestonline.com

It was a few weeks before our first Passion Test Certification program. One of the participants, Arnold Young, sent an e-mail saying, "I have an incredibly exciting idea to tell you about. I can't wait to see you at the certification training."

We thought, that's nice and didn't think much more about it.

Then, at the course, we met Arnold. It turns out Arnold's passion is software development. He told us how excited he got as he read *The Passion Test*, and he had started creating a software tool for himself to help him do the exercises and use the knowledge in the book to improve his own life.

He said, "I think I can create a program that will make the knowledge you've shared in the book come alive for people. We can make it so easy and so much fun for them to choose in favor of their passions. Plus, the program can automatically track their progress so they can see how they're doing."

While the idea sounded great, frankly, we are approached by people all the time with one great idea or another. Most of these great ideas fall short of their promise. Then, Arnold asked, "Will it be okay if I put together a prototype so you can see how it will work, and would you take half an hour on the phone to see what you think?"

We said, "Sure." Both of us were interested to see if and how Arnold would follow through.

Two weeks later he called. "I have the prototype ready. When can I get you both on the phone?" he asked.

That was easier said than done, but a few days later Janet was on the phone in an airport as she left for her next speaking engagement and Chris connected the three of us. Arnold walked us through his prototype, and frankly

we were blown away!

Arnold had taken every exercise in the book and created a simple, easy-to-use interface to complete them online. He even had a whole section for creating your Vision Board on your computer!

But here was the best part, Arnold had designed a "Passionometer" that takes your responses within the program and shows you how closely your life is aligning with your passions. How cool is that?

There is another powerful yet easy-to-use tool you can use anytime you're faced with a choice, a decision, or an opportunity. It will help you determine if that choice will help you get more aligned with your passions or take you away from your passions. Your Decision Meter will show you how well you're doing in staying aligned.

On top of that, Arnold's design was elegant and fun.

We enthusiastically said yes! And now The Passion Test Online is available to you for thirty days just by making a $2 donation. Your donation will help support Janet's projects with homeless women and youth in detention centers. After the first thirty days there is a modest monthly fee to keep using this powerful tool to stay on track.

Please don't close this book saying, "Wow, what a great book!" Though that would be flattering to us, what we *really* want is to help you take the next step and *turn your passion into a rewarding and fulfilling life.*

The Passion Test Online can help you put the principles you've learned into practice. Remember, "Action engages attention." So take action now, and sign up for your thirty-day trial at www.passiontestonline.com.

—Janet Bray Attwood and Chris Attwood

Offer subject to continuation of www.passiontestonline.com

How to Claim Your

Free Reports and Audio Recordings

When the story of your life is written, how will you feel about it? What you've learned in this book can transform your life only if you put it into practice. We invite you to start *living* the story of your dreams.

For this purpose, we have put together some of the systems and tools you'll need. You'll find them at:

www.thepassiontest.com/bookgifts.

After reading this book, we want you to feel connected to people and resources that can help you get massive results from what you've learned. Some of the gifts you'll get include:

Mark Victor Hansen Interviews Dr. Wayne Dyer

One of our best Passion Series interviews, Wayne shows you how to change your thinking and marshal the power of inspiration to realize your true calling in life.

Staying in Love: 7 Steps to an Open Heart and Mind

In this four-hour audio program you'll learn our seven-step expansion process that will show you how to stay in love with life and move gracefully through any change.

Speeding Up Your Success by Ten to Twenty Times

Marshall Thurber is a living genius in the tradition of his mentors, Nobel Laureate R. Buckminster Fuller and W. Edwards Deming. In this special report he teaches you the three cutting-edge business principles that transformed our business and how to apply them to yours.

These are only a few of the gifts waiting for you, so go get all of them now and begin *living* the story of your dreams.

To access free reports and recordings, users must register by providing their first name and an e-mail address. Offer subject to availability and author's continuation of www.thepassiontest.com.